LEVEL D

VOCABULARY

word meaning, pronunciation, prefixes, suffixes, synonyms, antonyms, and fun!

in Action

LOYOLA PRESS.

Chicago

LOYOLAPRESS.

3441 N. Ashland Avenue
Chicago, Illinois 60657
(800) 621-1008
www.loyolapress.com

Cover & Interior Art: Anni Betts
Cover Design: Judine O'Shea
Interior Design: Kathy Greenholdt

Manufactured in the United States of America.

ISBN-10: 0-8294-2772-4

ISBN-13: 978-0-8294-2772-1

16 17 Hess 10 9 8 6 7 5 4

Contents

Pronunciation Key iv

Pretest 1

Chapter 1 5
Chapter 2 17
   Review for Chapters 1 and 2 29

Chapter 3 31
Chapter 4 43
   Review for Chapters 3 and 4 55

Chapter 5 57
Chapter 6 69
   Review for Chapters 5 and 6 81

Posttest 83
Test-Taking Tips 89
Roots, Prefixes 91
Suffixes 92
Games & Activities 93

Index of Words 99

Pronunciation Key

This key shows the meanings of the abbreviations and symbols used throughout the book.

Some English words have more than one possible pronunciation. This book gives only one pronunciation per word, except when different pronunciations indicate different parts of speech. For example, when the word *relay* is used as a noun, it is pronounced rē´ lā; as a verb, the word is pronounced rə lā´.

Parts of Speech

adj.	adjective	*int.*	interjection	*prep.*	preposition
adv.	adverb	*n.*	noun	*part.*	participle
				v.	verb

Vowels

ā	tape	ə	about, circus	ôr	torn
a	map	ī	kite	oi	noise
âr	stare	i	win	ou	foul
ä	car, father	ō	toe	o͞o	soon
ē	meet	o	mop	o͝o	book
e	kept	ô	law	u	tug

Consonants

ch	check	ŋ	rang	y	yellow
g	girl	th	thimble	zh	treasure
j	jam	~~th~~	that	sh	shelf

Stress

The accent mark follows the syllable receiving the major stress, such as in the word *plaster* (plas´ tər).

Pretest

This test contains some of the words you will find in this book. It will give you an idea of the kinds of words you will study. When you have completed all the chapters, the posttest will measure what you have learned.

CHOOSING THE DEFINITIONS

Fill in the bubble of the item that best defines the word in bold in each sentence.

1. At night, the old house made **peculiar** sounds.
   a. loud   **b.** pleasant   **c.** familiar   **d.** strange

2. A **citizen** has the right to vote.
   a. village   **b.** resident   **c.** person   **d.** woman

3. From the **plateau**, we could see for miles.
   a. valley   **b.** border   **c.** highland   **d.** ocean

4. The baby was **bashful** around strangers.
   a. confident   **b.** shy   **c.** silly   **d.** sly

5. The crops grew tall in the **fertile** soil.
   a. rich   **b.** rocky   **c.** damp   **d.** dry

6. Mr. Mendez **exaggerated** the size of the fish he caught.
   a. belittled   **b.** shouted out   **c.** measured   **d.** magnified

7. The ranger shared useful **knowledge** about camping.
   a. tools   **b.** information   **c.** thoughts   **d.** rules

8. Work carefully so that you will not make an **error**.
   a. mistake   **b.** answer   **c.** project   **d.** step

9. The artist turned the **formless** lump of clay into a beautiful statue.
   a. hard   **b.** sculpted   **c.** heavy   **d.** unshaped

10. The umpire settled the **dispute** quickly.
    a. friendship   **b.** question   **c.** argument   **d.** agreement

11. Ayla did not want to **disappoint** her teammates.
    a. trust   **b.** go with   **c.** please   **d.** let down

12. Sleeping late on Saturday morning is a real **luxury**.
    a. expense   **b.** extra comfort   **c.** necessity   **d.** nap

13. The piano teacher played a sad **melody**.
    a. tune   **b.** story   **c.** speech   **d.** feeling

14. The new shoes are **exactly** the right size.
    a. almost   **b.** incorrectly   **c.** precisely   **d.** not

15. The whole family **relished** the food Dad grilled.
    a. cooked   **b.** disliked   **c.** enjoyed   **d.** served

16. Our new puppy **whined** when we left it alone.
    a. whimpered   **b.** barked   **c.** leaped   **d.** slept

17. The backyard was **disarranged** after the children's party.
    a. crowded   **b.** messy   **c.** empty   **d.** neat

18. Noah started a program to **recycle** used paper at his school.
    a. throw away   **b.** haul   **c.** use again   **d.** count

19. In her **haste** to catch the bus, Alexis forgot her lunch.
    a. fear   **b.** a heavy load   **c.** dislike   **d.** hurry

20. Many people come to the United States to find **liberty**.
    a. gold   **b.** freedom   **c.** adventure   **d.** homes

21. The artist placed the painting on the **easel**.
    a. frame   **b.** place   **c.** wall   **d.** stand

22. Victoria's **ancestors** lived in Peru.
    a. sisters   **b.** family founders   **c.** grandchildren   **d.** cousins

23. I enjoy living in our friendly **community**.
    a. apartment   **b.** neighborhood   **c.** house   **d.** country

24. They will build a new store on the **vacant** lot.
    a. weedy   **b.** crowded   **c.** empty   **d.** large

25. The law **forbids** skateboarding at the mall.
    a. does not allow   **b.** urges   **c.** allows   **d.** wants

26. I thought my brother broke the game, but he was **innocent**.
    a. happy   **b.** wrong   **c.** too young   **d.** not guilty

27. The chef prepared a **banquet** for the wedding guests.
    a. party favor   **b.** dessert   **c.** feast   **d.** snack

28. The new girl showed great athletic **ability**.
    a. clumsiness   **b.** talent   **c.** weakness   **d.** charm

29. My cousin is the **companion** I trust the most.
    a. teacher   **b.** doctor   **c.** teammate   **d.** friend

30. This medicine has a **horrid** smell.
    a. dreadful   **b.** pleasant   **c.** nice   **d.** flowery

31. In kindergarten, we vowed that our friendship would be **eternal.**
    a. very short   **b.** important   **c.** lasting forever   **d.** ordinary

32. The **flexible** hose easily bent around the corner.
    a. rubber   **b.** not stiff   **c.** rigid   **d.** garden

33. It took the hikers all day to reach the bottom of the **canyon.**
    a. hill   **b.** stream   **c.** frozen ground   **d.** deep valley

34. The teacher **demonstrated** how to stop on skis.
    a. showed   **b.** understood   **c.** recorded   **d.** learned

35. The snow looks so bright because it **reflects** the sun's rays.
    a. blocks   **b.** dims   **c.** throws back   **d.** cools down

36. Platinum is valuable because it is **scarce.**
    a. plentiful   **b.** beautiful   **c.** rare   **d.** old

37. Let's **reorganize** my video game library.
    a. clean out   **b.** arrange again   **c.** fill up   **d.** close again

38. The viceroy butterfly **masquerades** as the monarch butterfly.
    a. disguises itself   **b.** flies   **c.** has a cocoon   **d.** eats

39. We learned all about the **geography** of Australia.
    a. animals   **b.** language   **c.** people   **d.** land

40. The flood knocked the house off its **foundation.**
    a. driveway   **b.** base   **c.** floor   **d.** roof

41. In an address you can **abbreviate** Massachusetts to MA.
    a. spell   **b.** leave out   **c.** shorten   **d.** divide

42. His apology sounded **sincere** to me.
    a. real   **b.** loud   **c.** dishonest   **d.** sad

43. The woolly **garment** felt warm but scratchy.
    a. lamb   **b.** rug   **c.** clothing   **d.** sack

44. The climber heard an **echo** as his words bounced off the mountain.
    a. whisper   **b.** shout   **c.** song   **d.** repetition

45. The president made a difficult **decision.**
    a. choice   **b.** agreement   **c.** argument   **d.** idea

46. Our class saw ancient mummies and dinosaur bones at the **museum.**
   a. theater   **b.** exhibit hall   **c.** stadium   **d.** school

47. The insects were so tiny they were almost **invisible.**
   a. bright   **b.** strong   **c.** miniature   **d.** unseen

48. The **journey** through the desert was long, hot, and difficult.
   a. adventure   **b.** trip   **c.** road   **d.** river

49. The rich **merchant** displayed colorful rugs.
   a. trader   **b.** farmer   **c.** sailor   **d.** lawyer

50. It is hard to succeed as a **professional** musician.
   a. amateur   **b.** part-time   **c.** expert   **d.** untrained

51. The hair on the old bear's **snout** was turning gray.
   a. chin   **b.** nose and mouth   **c.** back and legs   **d.** tail

52. A careful **consumer** always compares prices.
   a. buyer   **b.** mechanic   **c.** producer   **d.** reader

53. You can buy a used computer for a **fraction** of the original cost.
   a. total   **b.** breakdown   **c.** explanation   **d.** part

54. The weight lifter was **capable** of lifting 400 pounds.
   a. heavy   **b.** able   **c.** unfit   **d.** allowed to

55. Firefighters must act quickly in an **emergency.**
   a. fire   **b.** crisis   **c.** practice   **d.** vehicle

56. Micah's work was **satisfactory**, so he received a small raise.
   a. bad   **b.** difficult   **c.** acceptable   **d.** fun

57. It takes hard work and good luck to **forecast** weather correctly.
   a. predict   **b.** ignore   **c.** wait for   **d.** prepare for

58. The long wait for tickets made the spectators **impatient.**
   a. peaceful   **b.** restless   **c.** happy   **d.** cold

59. You do not need to understand a computer's **operation** to use one.
   a. moving parts   **b.** repair   **c.** engine   **d.** workings

60. An ordinary trip to the store turned into a great **adventure.**
   a. bad weather   **b.** vacation   **c.** project   **d.** exciting experience

CHAPTER 1

WORD LIST

Read each word using the pronunciation key.

Group A

adventure (ad ven´ chər)
capable (kā´ pə bəl)
conduct (*v.* kən dukt´) (*n.* kon´ dukt)
demonstrate (dem´ ən strāt)
escort (*n.* es´ kôrt) (*v.* es kôrt´)
eternal (i tərn´ əl)
industrious (in dus´ trē əs)
insulation (in sə lā´ shən)
peculiar (pi kyo͞ol´ yər)
respect (ri spekt´)

Group B

ability (ə bil´ ə tē)
callus (kal´ əs)
community (kə myo͞o´ nə tē)
dependable (di pen´ də bəl)
exactly (ig zak´ tlē)
hospitality (hos pə tal´ ə tē)
knowledge (näl´ ij)
pledge (pledj)
sensible (sen´ sə bəl)
sincere (sin sēr´)

WORD STUDY

Prefixes

The prefix *pre-* means "before."

precook (prē ko͞ok´) (*v.*) to cook for eating later
premature (prē mə chur´) (*adj.*) before the correct time
prepay (prē pā´) (*v.*) to pay in advance
preschool (prē´ sko͞ol) (*n.*) a school for children younger than those attending elementary school
prerecord (prē rē kôrd´) (*v.*) to record in advance for later use
preview (prē´ vyoo) (*n.*) an advance showing, such as of a movie, play, or TV program

Challenge Words

abominate (ə bom´ ə nāt)
confide (kən fīd´)
extravagant (ek stra´ və gənt)
forlorn (fôr lôrn´)
interval (in´ tər vəl)

Read each sentence below to figure out the meaning of the word in **bold**. Use reasoning skills and the remainder of the sentence to help you. Write the meaning of the word on the line.

1. Some people in our **community** are planning a town festival.

_____

2. The hikers stayed on the trail; they have **respect** for nature.

_____

3. There is a **peculiar** smell coming from the old refrigerator.

_____

4. The princess and her **escort** danced until midnight.

_____

5. The team always arrives **exactly** 30 minutes before the game.

_____

6. An **industrious** group of scouts will help rebuild the damaged homes.

_____

7. Dependable members of the group pick up highway litter every week—rain or shine.

_____

8. Jacob and Emily **pledge** to spend time each day practicing their trumpets.

_____

9. The professor shared his firsthand **knowledge** with our class.

_____

10. The **sensible** thing to do is to call the store before you go.

_____

WORD MEANINGS

Word Learning—Group A

Study the spelling, part(s) of speech, and meaning(s) of each word from Group A. Complete each sentence by writing the word on the line. Then read the sentence.

1. adventure *(n.)* an unusual or exciting experience involving some risk

The hike to Machu Picchu was a thrilling _____.

2. capable *(adj.)* 1. able; 2. having the physical fitness, power, or ability to do something

The plumber is _____ of doing her job well.

3. conduct *(v.)* to guide, manage, or direct; *(n.)* a way of behaving

The usher will _____ you to your seat.

Others will be observing your _____.

4. demonstrate *(v.)* 1. to explain by using examples; 2. to show clearly; 3. to prove

Who will _____ how the MP3 player works?

5. escort *(n.)* a person or group going with another to give protection or as a courtesy; *(v.)* to go with someone to provide protection

The rock star's _____ is following her.

The police will _____ the president to the monument.

6. eternal *(adj.)* 1. lasting forever; 2. endless

John F. Kennedy's memorial is marked by an _____ flame.

7. industrious *(adj.)* working hard and regularly

An _____ group of students built a robot.

8. insulation *(n.)* 1. barrier; 2. something that prevents heat loss

Our house is warmer with new _____.

9. peculiar *(adj.)* 1. out of the ordinary; 2. distinct; 3. unusual

The armadillo appears to be a _____ animal.

10. respect *(v.)* 1. to show honor; 2. to think highly of; *(n.)* 1. care;
2. consideration

We _____ the opinions of our friends.

Your _____ for other readers is appreciated in the library.

Use Your Vocabulary—Group A

Choose the word from Group A that best completes each sentence. Write the word on the line. You may use the plural form of nouns and the past tense of verbs if necessary.

Would you __1__ me to the baseball game?
I'm __2__ of going to the ballpark myself, but I'd
like you to go with me. Besides, I know that
you will be good company and will
__3__ yourself well. There are a lot of busy
and __4__ vendors in the stands. I have
__5__ for the peanut vendors who make their
job look like fun. Let's ask the peanut man
to __6__ his superduper peanut throw into
the back row. That was a very __7__ over-the-
shoulder, behind-the-back, peanut bag toss. I
think the ice-cream vendor is using mounds
of popcorn for __8__ to keep the ice cream cold
on this hot day. A slow baseball game would
seem __9__ if it weren't for the funny vendors.
Too bad our team lost the game, but we still
had a memorable __10__ .

1. _____

2. _____

3. _____

4. _____

5. _____

6. _____

7. _____

8. _____

9. _____

10. _____

Notable Quotes

"If you once forfeit the confidence of your fellow citizens, you can never regain their **respect** and esteem. It is true that you may fool all of the people some of the time; you can even fool some of the people all of the time; but you can't fool all of the people all of the time."

—Abraham Lincoln (1809–1865), 16th president of United States

Word Learning—Group B

Study the spelling, part(s) of speech, and meaning(s) of each word from Group B. Complete each sentence by writing the word on the line. Then read the sentence.

1. ability *(n.)* 1. skill or talent; 2. power to perform a task

Michael's _____ to fix cars keeps my old junker running.

2. callus *(n.)* thickened area of the skin

Your tight shoes caused this _____ on your foot.

3. community *(n.)* all the people living in the same area

All the neighbors helped build the park for this _____.

4. dependable *(adj.)* 1. able to be trusted; 2. reliable; 3. responsible

Our Citizen of the Year award goes to a very _____ person.

5. exactly *(adv.)* 1. without any mistake; 2. precisely

Place the vase of flowers _____ in the middle of the table.

6. hospitality *(n.)* the friendly treatment of guests or strangers

This restaurant is famous for its good food and _____.

7. knowledge *(n.)* 1. what a person knows; 2. information

His _____ of music made the concert more interesting.

8. pledge *(n.)* a genuine promise; *(v.)* 1. to give as security; 2. to agree to do; 3. to vow

I need your _____ to help me raise the money.

I _____ allegiance to the flag of the United States of America.

9. sensible *(adj.)* 1. showing good sense or judgment; 2. wise

It was a simple yet _____ solution to our problem.

10. sincere *(adj.)* 1. honest; 2. real; 3. genuine

Hannah made a _____ attempt to repay the money.

Use Your Vocabulary—Group B

Choose the word from Group B that best completes each sentence. Write the word on the line. You may use the plural form of nouns and the past tense of verbs if necessary.

I made a(n) __1__ to myself to learn something new this year. There are free bowling lessons for kids in my __2__ every Saturday. I think this would be a(n) __3__ choice for me because it's easy, free, and I can use my sister's bowling ball. I hope the bowling shoes don't give me a(n) __4__ on my foot. I can count on my __5__ friend, Rosa, to bowl with me. We will be good bowling partners because we have the same __6__, though our combined __7__ of the sport does not add up to much! To be fair, Rosa does know a little bit more than I do. She knows __8__ how to keep score. I am very __9__ in my promise to work hard and learn how to do that too. But even if Rosa and I never become good bowlers, we will still enjoy the kind __10__ of the owners of the bowling alley.

1. _____
2. _____
3. _____
4. _____
5. _____
6. _____
7. _____
8. _____
9. _____
10. _____

Vocabulary in Action

The rules of **hospitality** in the ancient Middle East were very important. In desert climates, food and water were often scarce. Homes and villages were often built near the only water source for many miles. Strict rules arose about taking care of travelers, foreigners, and strangers. If a stranger knocked on your door and asked for food, water, or a place to sleep, you were expected to provide it. To refuse was to break a sacred code that everyone lived by.

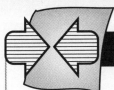

SYNONYMS

Synonyms are words that have the same or nearly the same meanings.

Part 1 Choose the word from the box that is the best synonym for each group of words. Write the word on the line.

industrious	knowledge	respect	community	conduct
capable	adventure	eternal	hospitality	escort

1. admire; consideration   _____

2. guide, direct; behavior   _____

3. city, group, neighborhood   _____

4. fit, able, competent   _____

5. everlasting, undying   _____

6. experience, voyage, journey   _____

7. friendliness, generosity   _____

8. bodyguard; go with, protect   _____

9. hardworking, busy, diligent   _____

10. learning, information, wisdom   _____

Notable Quotes

"The best thing to give to your enemy is forgiveness; to an opponent, tolerance; to a friend, your heart; to your child, a good example; to a father, deference; to your mother, **conduct** that will make her proud of you; to yourself, respect; to all men, charity."

—Benjamin Franklin (1706–1790), author, inventor, statesman, founding father of United States

Part 2 Replace the underlined word(s) with a word from the box that means the same or almost the same. Write your answer on the line.

sincere	peculiar	callus	ability	insulation
pledge	sensible	demonstrate	exactly	dependable

11. His <u>skill</u> in gymnastics won him a gold medal. _____

12. The husband and wife made a <u>promise</u> to save more money.

   _____

13. The <u>lining</u> around the wire protects us from electrical shock.

   _____

14. Make each answer as <u>reasonable</u> as you can. _____

15. Let me <u>show you</u> how to use the lawn mower. _____

16. Matt cut the board <u>correctly</u> to the measurements. _____

17. The city bus is <u>reliable</u> transportation. _____

18. He gave us his <u>honest</u> opinion about our work. _____

19. No one noticed the <u>odd</u> color of his hair. _____

20. I grip my tennis racket so tightly that I now have a <u>patch of hard skin</u>

   on my thumb. _____

Vocabulary in Action

The **pledge** you probably know best is the Pledge of Allegiance to the U.S. flag. This pledge was written in 1892 by Francis Bellamy. You may not know that the Pledge of Allegiance has changed a few times since it was written. The original Pledge read, "I pledge allegiance to my Flag and the Republic for which it stands: one Nation indivisible, with Liberty and Justice for all." How does that compare with today's Pledge?

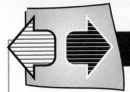

ANTONYMS

Antonyms are words that have opposite or nearly opposite meanings.

| exactly | knowledge | eternal |
| capable | sincere | ability |

Part 1 Choose the word from the box that is the best antonym for each group of words. Write the word on the line.

1. false, dishonest, deceptive _____

2. weakness, incapacity _____

3. ignorance, stupidity, inexperience _____

4. sloppily, inaccurately, generally _____

5. unable, unfit _____

6. passing, comes to an end, temporary _____

Part 2 Replace the underlined word with a word from the box that means the opposite or almost the opposite. Write your answer on the line.

| peculiar | industrious | dependable |
| respect | hospitality | sensible |

7. The night guard keeps <u>normal</u> working hours. _____

8. The colonel retired from the army with <u>dishonor</u>. _____

9. The welcoming committee was known for its <u>rudeness</u>.

_____

10. Kai's mother wore an <u>impractical</u> suit to the office. _____

11. The workers had an <u>idle</u> day at the factory. _____

12. Our <u>unreliable</u> washing machine began to shake. _____

WORD STUDY

Prefixes Write an answer for each statement in the space provided. Then choose a word from the box below and include it in your sentence.

| precook | premature | prepay |
| preschool | prerecord | preview |

1. Name something that you did before you started elementary school.

   _____ Write a sentence about it.

   _____

2. Name two things you can cook to eat at a later time.

   _____   _____

   Write a sentence about one of them.

   _____

3. Name something that you can pay for in advance.

   _____ Write a sentence about it.

   _____

4. Name two things you would like to record to watch or listen to later.

   _____   _____

   Write a sentence about one of them.

   _____

5. Name a movie or TV program for which you saw an advance showing.

   _____ Write a sentence about what you saw.

   _____

6. Name something that can happen too soon.

   _____ Write a sentence about it.

   _____

CHALLENGE WORDS

Word Learning—Challenge!

Study the spelling, part(s) of speech, and meaning(s) of each word. Complete each sentence by writing the word on the line. Then read the sentence.

1. **abominate** *(v.)* to hate

   People who are trying to sleep _____ loud noises.

2. **confide** *(v.)* 1. to tell as a secret; 2. to show trust

   My best friend likes to _____ her secrets to me.

3. **extravagant** *(adj.)* 1. carelessly spending too much; 2. wasteful

   A solid gold toothbrush is an _____ birthday present.

4. **forlorn** *(adj.)* 1. lonely; 2. miserable; 3. hopeless; neglected

   A cat in the rain looks sad and _____.

5. **interval** *(n.)* a time or space between things

   There will be a 15-minute _____ between the first and second acts of the play.

Use Your Vocabulary–Challenge!

Goose on the Loose A goose wearing a diamond collar gets loose on the field during a baseball game. The players try different ways to catch it, but fail. Finally, one player has an idea that works. On a separate sheet of paper, write a news story about the incident. Use the Challenge Words above. Be sure to answer the questions *who, what, where, why,* and *when.*

> ### Vocabulary in Action
>
> A way to remember the meaning of **confide** is to think about the word *confidence,* which means "the quality or state of being certain." A person is more likely to confide in someone if he or she is certain that person can be trusted. Since the two words are so closely related, this trick may be easy to remember.

FUN WITH WORDS

The questions below use vocabulary words from this chapter. Write your answer to each question on the line.

1. Who is the person that you most *respect*? _____

2. Does this person live in your *community*? _____

3. Would you say that this person is *industrious*? Why?

_____

_____

4. What other qualities does this person *demonstrate*?

_____

_____

5. In what area might this person have a lot of *knowledge*?

_____

_____

6. What special skill or *ability* does this person have?

_____

_____

7. Do you want to be *exactly* like this person? Explain your answer.

_____

_____

8. How could you *conduct* yourself to be more like this person?

_____

CHAPTER 2

WORD LIST

Read each word using the pronunciation key.

Group A

abbreviate (ə brē´ vē āt)
capital (kap´ ət əl)
decay (di kā´)
emergency (i mər´ jən sē)
financial (fə nan´ chəl)
garment (gär´ mənt)
innocent (in´ ə sənt)
magnet (mag´ nət)
obedient (ō bē´ dē ənt)
whirl (hwərl)

Group B

canal (kə nal´)
canyon (kan´ yən)
draft (draft)
error (er´ ər)
evaporate (i vap´ ə rāt)
fertile (fərt´ l)
journey (jər´ nē)
molar (mō´ lər)
recycle (rē sī´ kəl)
snout (snout)

WORD STUDY

Suffixes

The suffix -*able* means "able to be" or "full of."

agreeable (ə grē´ ə bəl) *(adj.)* able to agree
comfortable (kəmf´ tə bəl) *(adj.)* full of comfort
enjoyable (in joi´ ə bəl) *(adj.)* full of joy
reasonable (rē´ zən ə bəl) *(adj.)* able to reason
valuable (val´ yə bəl) *(adj.)* full of value
washable (wash´ ə bəl) *(adj.)* able to be washed

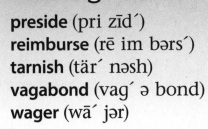

Challenge Words

preside (pri zīd´)
reimburse (rē im bərs´)
tarnish (tär´ nəsh)
vagabond (vag´ ə bond)
wager (wā´ jər)

WORDS IN CONTEXT

Read each sentence below to figure out the meaning of the word in **bold**. Use reasoning skills and the remainder of the sentence to help you. Write the meaning of the word on the line.

1. Our social studies class took a bus to the **capital** of our state to meet the governor.

   _____

2. We are moving closer to the city so that Dad's **journey** to work won't be so long.

   _____

3. The view from the house on the hill overlooks a **canyon**.

   _____

4. The best corn and soybeans are grown in the **fertile** soil of the Midwest.

   _____

5. Boatloads of people traveled on the **canal** before the railroad was built.

   _____

6. Who found this cute puppy with the long ears and short **snout**?

   _____

7. I would like my dog to be **obedient** when I command it to "sit."

   _____

8. Be sure to **recycle** your used newspapers, cans, and bottles.

   _____

9. My mom is now in a **financial** position to own her own business.

   _____

10. Use the **magnet** to post your A+ math paper on the refrigerator.

    _____

WORD MEANINGS

Word Learning—Group A

Study the spelling, part(s) of speech, and meaning(s) of each word from Group A. Complete each sentence by writing the word on the line. Then read the sentence.

1. abbreviate *(v.)* to shorten

When writing a letter, you may _____ the title Doctor.

2. capital *(n.)* a city where a country or state's government is located; *(adj.)* most important

The _____ of Texas is Austin.

The _____ ships in the fleet were the most heavily protected.

3. decay *(v.)* to rot or spoil; *(n.)* a decrease in power, strength, or beauty

As the fallen leaves _____, they make new soil.

Bad leadership can lead to the _____ of a government's power.

4. emergency *(n.)* need for quick action; *(adj.)* for a time of sudden need

The paramedics responded to the medical _____.

The patient was taken to the hospital's _____ room.

5. financial *(adj.)* relating to or dealing with money

Saving money can improve your _____ situation.

6. garment *(n.)* piece of clothing

I want to wear a new _____ to the wedding.

7. innocent *(adj.)* 1. doing no wrong or evil; 2. free from guilt or blame

The jury believed that the senator was _____ of the crime.

8. magnet *(n.)* a piece of metal that attracts iron

Anna's refrigerator is covered with souvenir _____.

9. obedient *(adj.)* doing what one is told to do

Our old golden retriever is a loyal and _____ dog.

10. whirl *(v.)* 1. to turn or swing in a circle; 2. to spin

We watched the merry-go-round _____ around and around.

Use Your Vocabulary—Group A

Choose the word from Group A that best completes each sentence. Write the word on the line. You may use the plural form of nouns and the past tense of verbs if necessary.

Let's take my car for a(n) __1__ around the streets of the state __2__ . We need to be __3__ when it comes to the traffic laws. If we get stopped for a ticket, we may have to __4__ our tour, which is already too short. Let's go to the shopping district where fine __5__ are sold. It is an old part of town. Some buildings have __6__ , but there are plans to restore many of them. The old bookstores draw me in like a(n) __7__ and tempt me to spend even my __8__ funds. If we run out of cash, we'll just head to the __9__ district, where all the banks are located. I hope my wife will believe that I am __10__ of overspending.

1. _____

2. _____

3. _____

4. _____

5. _____

6. _____

7. _____

8. _____

9. _____

10. _____

Word Learning—Group B

Study the spelling, part(s) of speech, and meaning(s) of each word from Group B. Complete each sentence by writing the word on the line. Then read the sentence.

1. **canal** *(n.)* human-made waterway

   The boats traveled between the two cities on the narrow

   _____.

2. **canyon** *(n.)* deep valley

   The campers hiked to the bottom of the _____.

3. **draft** *(n.)* current of air; *(v.)* to make a rough copy or sketch of

   Please block the cold _____ coming through the window.

   Would you edit the first _____ of my essay?

4. **error** *(n.)* mistake

   Take a moment to correct the _____ in this paragraph.

5. **evaporate** *(v.)* to dry up or disappear

   The water will _____ when you heat it.

6. **fertile** *(adj.)* able to produce seeds, fruit, or young

   The farmer planted a _____ field with tomatoes and beans.

7. **journey** *(n.)* 1. travel from one place to another; 2. a trip; *(v.)* to travel

   Bob and Carol are planning a _____ around the world.

   They will _____ through Europe, Asia, and North America.

8. **molar** *(n.)* tooth used for grinding

   Her toddler's new _____ is coming in nicely.

9. **recycle** *(v.)* to process something so that it may be used again

   _____ all the empty aluminum cans.

10. snout *(n.)* part of an animal that contains the nose, mouth, and jaws

The muzzle goes around the watchdog's _____.

Use Your Vocabulary—Group B

Choose the word from Group B that best completes each sentence. Write the word on the line. You may use the plural form of nouns and the past tense of verbs if necessary.

I took a(n) __1__ by boat through the countryside. I traveled by way of a(n) __2__. The views of green, __3__ farmlands were relaxing. I felt my worries __4__ like water on a hot day. My boat was followed for a mile or so by a sheep dog with white feet and a black __5__. His smile was so wide that I could see the __6__ at the back of his jaw. His thick fur looked to be good at keeping out the cold __7__ of winter, but I bet he was uncomfortable on this warm day. I crumpled my drink can and threw it into a bin to be __8__. I remembered then that I had almost decided to hike deep into the western __9__ on my vacation this year. That would have been a huge __10__. I needed this clear air and lazy pace to restore my energy and make me feel whole again!

1. _____

2. _____

3. _____

4. _____

5. _____

6. _____

7. _____

8. _____

9. _____

10. _____

Vocabulary in Action

A way to remember the meaning of **error** is to think about the word *erratic*, which means "lacking consistency or uniformity." A person is more likely to make an error if his or her actions lack consistency or uniformity. Since both words begin with *err*, this trick may be easy to remember.

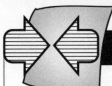

SYNONYMS

Synonyms are words that have the same or nearly the same meanings.

Part 1 Choose the word from the box that is the best synonym for each group of words. Write the word on the line.

obedient	error	capital	financial	canyon
magnet	innocent	emergency	recycle	garment

1. blameless, faultless, pure   _____

2. crisis; suddenly needed   _____

3. dress, apparel, clothing   _____

4. gorge, valley, ravine   _____

5. important, chief, supreme   _____

6. metal that attracts   _____

7. loyal, devoted, willing   _____

8. mistake, blunder, blooper   _____

9. money-related, economic   _____

10. use again   _____

Notable Quotes

"The wonders of the Grand **Canyon** cannot be adequately represented in symbols of speech nor by speech itself. The resources of the graphic art are taxed beyond their powers in attempting to portray its features . . . The glories and beauties of form, color, and sound unite in the Grand Canyon."

—John Wesley Powell (1834–1902),
explorer, geologist, soldier

Part 2 Replace the underlined word(s) with a word from the box that means the same or almost the same. Write your answer on the line.

journey	fertile	canal	whirl	molar
snout	decay	abbreviate	draft	evaporate

11. Gently hold Roscoe's <u>muzzle</u> closed so he'll swallow the pill.

_____

12. The best oranges are grown in the <u>rich</u> soil of this valley.

_____

13. The ripe vegetables in the stalled truck began to <u>rot</u> in the hot

sun. _____

14. Write state names in full; do not <u>shorten</u> them. _____

15. Here's our first <u>version</u> of the script for this year's Thanksgiving

Day play. _____

16. The dancers will <u>spin</u> faster as the music gets louder.

_____

17. Be sure to brush each <u>back tooth</u>. _____

18. Don't let your dreams <u>disappear</u> when things get difficult.

_____

19. Austin showed us photographs from his <u>voyage</u> to the Great Barrier

Reef. _____

20. Our barge cruise takes us through an old shipping <u>channel</u> in France.

_____

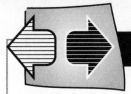

ANTONYMS

Antonyms are words that have opposite or nearly opposite meanings.

Part 1 Choose the word from the box that is the best antonym for each group of words. Write the word on the line.

| error | canyon | abbreviate | fertile | decay |

1. peak, mountaintop, highland _____

2. correctness, accuracy _____

3. grow, flourish, strengthen _____

4. sterile, barren, not productive _____

5. lengthen, extend, spell out _____

Part 2 Replace the underlined word(s) with a word from the box that means the opposite or almost the opposite. Write your answer on the line.

| draft | recycle | obedient | innocent | capital |

6. "All evidence points to the fact that this man is <u>guilty</u>," said the lawyer. _____

7. The senator proclaimed the president's plan as a <u>trivial</u> idea.

   _____

8. Can anyone here <u>finalize</u> the written portion of our report?

   _____

9. The young actor was <u>defiant</u> whenever the director told him what

   to do. _____

10. Wait! Don't <u>throw away</u> yesterday's newspapers until I've read them.

    _____

WORD STUDY

Suffixes Write the word from the box below that best completes each of the following sentences.

agreeable	comfortable	enjoyable
reasonable	valuable	washable

1. The cotton blanket is _____, but the wool blanket is not.

2. My baseball card collection is _____, and I'm going to sell it.

3. The committee was _____ to your idea and voted yes.

4. The good dinner and interesting company made for a(n) _____ evening.

5. Please sit in this cozy and _____ chair.

6. The rule that says you must be on time for class is _____.

Vocabulary in Action

People sometimes use the word **vagabond** to mean someone who is homeless or impoverished. But the word simply refers to someone who wanders from place to place. It comes from a Latin word that means "to wander."

CHALLENGE WORDS

Word Learning–Challenge!

Study the spelling, part(s) of speech, and meaning(s) of each word below. Complete each sentence by writing the word on the line. Then read the sentence.

1. preside *(v.)* to hold the place of authority

A new judge will _____ in traffic court today.

2. reimburse *(v.)* to pay back to someone

Please _____ me five dollars for the phone calls you made.

3. tarnish *(v.)* 1. to dull the luster of; 2. to bring disgrace on; *(n.)* a dull coating, especially on silver

If I'm caught committing a crime, it will _____ my reputation.

You can remove the _____ from a silver spoon by polishing it.

4. vagabond *(n.)* person who moves from place to place; *(adj.)* wandering

We call my uncle a _____ because he never lives in one place for long.

The _____ sailor kept sailing from one continent to another.

5. wager *(v.)* to make a bet; *(n.)* the act of betting

Did they _____ their money on the winner or the loser?

If you lose this _____, it will cost you money.

Use Your Vocabulary—Challenge!

Vacation Race Bailey bets Seth that she can ride across Arizona on her bike in six weeks. If she wins, Seth will pay her expenses. On a separate sheet of paper, write a story about Bailey's trip. Use the Challenge Words above. Be sure to tell what happens during the trip and who wins the bet.

FUN WITH WORDS

Find the 18 misspelled vocabulary words and underline them. Then spell each word correctly on the lines below the letter.

Dear Gavin,

What a week! It started with an emergincy meeting to talk about how to recycel all the farm's newspapers and cans. I made an inocent suggestion that no one liked, so I whurled out of the room. I was not paying attention as I walked down the path, and I almost fell into the caynon. Fortunately, my dog, Barker, was with me. He grabbed me with his snaut and pulled me to safety. He's such a good, obediente dog.

But that's not all. Tuesday the smell of decaiy came floating through my window with a drapht. I looked out to see that the water in the cannal had all evapporated. My once fertil garden was quickly dying. I threw on some garmints and rushed to buy hoses. Alas, my finanshal situation is not good, so I could only buy one watering can instead. I have been watering plants nonstop for three days. My arms and legs ache, and I believe even my molers are starting to get tired!

Perhaps it was an errer to move so far away from the city. I thought it was a capitle idea at first, but now I'm not so sure. What do you think I should do? Could you jurney to see me? I'd love to have you even for a few days. And I promise there will be no more disasters!

Best wishes,
Diana

_____   _____

_____   _____

_____   _____

_____   _____

_____   _____

_____   _____

_____   _____

_____   _____

Review 1–2

WORD MEANINGS

Fill in the bubble of the word that is best defined by each phrase.

1. odd, strange, unique
 a. industrious **b.** obedient   **c.** peculiar   **d.** capable

2. a talent or skill
 a. insulation   **b.** garment   **c.** error   **d.** ability

3. having the power or ability to do something
 a. capable   **b.** fertile   **c.** financial   **d.** sensible

4. precisely, without a mistake
 a. exactly   **b.** sincere   **c.** dependable   **d.** emergency

5. decrease or decline in power or beauty
 a. evaporate   **b.** molar   **c.** recycle   **d.** decay

6. to make shorter
 a. conduct   **b.** abbreviate   **c.** whirl   **d.** draft

7. to make a sketch or rough copy of
 a. demonstrate **b.** journey   **c.** draft   **d.** evaporate

8. a lowland or deep valley
 a. whirl   **b.** canal   **c.** canyon   **d.** molar

9. not guilty, doing no wrong
 a. innocent   **b.** industrious   **c.** dependable   **d.** capable

10. a hard place on the skin
 a. callus   **b.** molar   **c.** canyon   **d.** conduct

11. unending, lasting forever
 a. fertile   **b.** dependable   **c.** sensible   **d.** eternal

12. human-made waterway or river
 a. pledge   **b.** capital   **c.** canyon   **d.** canal

13. blunder, mistake
 a. error   **b.** molar   **c.** emergency   **d.** escort

14. a time of sudden need
 a. emergency   **b.** adventure   **c.** capital   **d.** community

15. having good sense or judgment
 a. sincere   **b.** sensible   **c.** obedient   **d.** industrious

SENTENCE COMPLETION

Choose the word from Part 1 that best completes each of the following sentences. Write the word in the blank. Then do the same for Part 2. You will not use all the words.

Part 1

insulation	knowledge	adventures	community
capital	garments	dependable	magnets

1. Let's listen to Harriet tell about her _____ as a storm chaser.

2. Property taxes are the _____ item on the agenda.

3. Our _____ is known for welcoming new neighbors.

4. If our home had better _____, we could save money on our heating bills.

5. The actor's _____ looked like they were from the time of Ancient Egypt.

Part 2

sincere	journey	pledged	conduct
hospitality	demonstrated	escorted	evaporate

6. We want to _____ to Panama this summer.

7. The people of Mexico are famous for welcoming guests to their country with great _____.

8. The lawyers _____ themselves in a serious way.

9. In Amsterdam, a police officer _____ me back to the library when I got lost.

10. The students _____ how oxygen is needed to keep a candle burning.

CHAPTER 3

WORD LIST

Read each word using the pronunciation key.

Group A

bashful (bash´ fəl)
charity (châr´ ə tē)
consumer (kən sōō mər)
formless (fôrm´ lis)
liberty (lib´ ər tē)
luxury (luk´ shə rē)
precious (presh´ əs)
relish (rel´ ish)
satisfactory (sat is fak´ tə rē)
transport (*v.* trans pôrt´)
      (*n.* trans´ pôrt)

Group B

allegiance (ə lē ´ jəns)
chemical (kem´ i kəl)
climate (klī´ mət)
equator (i kwāt´ ər)
galaxy (gal´ ək sē)
geography (jē äg´ rə fē)
horizon (hə rī´ zən)
invisible (in viz´ ə bəl)
prey (prā)
reflect (ri flekt´)

WORD STUDY

Homophones

Homophones are words that have the same pronunciation, but a different meaning and spelling.

piece (pēs) *(n.)* one of the parts into which a thing is divided
peace (pēs) *(n.)* freedom from war

waste (wāst) *(v.)* to make poor use of; to spend uselessly
waist (wāst) *(n.)* the part of the human body between the ribs and the hips

aisle (īl) *(n.)* passage between rows of seats
isle (īl) *(n.)* a small island

Challenge Words

aroma (ə rō´ mə)
deface (di fās´)
dismantle (dis man´ təl)
enlighten (in lī´ tən)
obstinate (ob´ stə nit)

WORDS IN CONTEXT

Read each sentence below to figure out the meaning of the word in **bold**. Use reasoning skills and the remainder of the sentence to help you. Write the meaning of the word on the line.

1. I felt **bashful** about meeting the other students in my new class.

_____

2. My softball team raised money for a **charity**.

_____

3. You might think Arizona temperatures are always warm, but the winter **climate** of northern Arizona calls for coats and sweaters.

_____

4. My uncle, a thrifty **consumer**, always uses coupons when he shops.

_____

5. The freedom-loving, revolutionary statesman Patrick Henry said, "Give me **liberty** or give me death."

_____

6. I wish I could be **invisible** so that I could sneak unseen into the opposing team's locker room and listen to their plans.

_____

7. Joshua used his birthday money to buy a **luxury** for himself—a gold-plated motorcycle with extra large tires.

_____

8. After months of being sick in bed, Jake **relished** the idea of going out.

_____

9. Christopher Columbus believed the earth was round because he saw boats sail over the **horizon** into the morning sun.

_____

10. When I mixed the **chemicals** in science class, the lab filled with smoke.

_____

WORD MEANINGS

Word Learning—Group A

Study the spelling, part(s) of speech, and meaning(s) of each word from Group A. Complete each sentence by writing the word on the line. Then read the sentence.

1. **bashful** *(adj.)* uneasy around others; shy

   The little boy flashed a _____ grin from behind his mother.

2. **charity** *(n.)* a generous giving to those who are poor, ill, or otherwise in need

   The Salvation Army bell ringers are collecting coins for

   _____.

3. **consumer** *(n.)* a buyer and a user of goods and services

   A careful _____ compares prices before buying a new car.

4. **formless** *(adj.)* having no regular form or shape

   A _____ blob is the monster in my favorite science-fiction movie.

5. **liberty** *(n.)* freedom; the right or power to do as one chooses

   The high school students have the _____ to leave school for lunch.

6. **luxury** *(n.)* 1. extra comfort; 2. beauties of life beyond what is necessary

   Let's snuggle in the _____ of a warm down comforter.

7. **precious** *(adj.)* of great value; cherished

   My great-grandmother's ring is a _____ family keepsake.

8. **relish** *(n.)* strong-flavored food that adds taste to other food; *(v.)* 1. to like the flavor of; 2. to like or enjoy

   Put some pickle _____ on my hot dog.

   I sure do _____ the taste of a sweet, ripe strawberry.

9. satisfactory *(adj.)* good enough to fulfill desires, hopes, demands

We didn't pass our goal, but we raised a _____ amount of money for the school.

10. transport *(v.)* to carry from one place to another; *(n.)* the act of bringing something from one place to another

The truck driver said he will _____ your furniture.

The boxes shifted in the truck during the _____.

Use Your Vocabulary—Group A

Choose the word from Group A that best completes each sentence. Write the word on the line. You may use the plural form of nouns and the past tense of verbs if necessary.

Many slaves had barely enough necessities to live and didn't dream of __1__. Some people wanted to end slavery and give __2__ to the slaves. But until the Emancipation Proclamation, they could only __3__ the thought of freedom for all. The Underground Railroad, which seemed to be __4__, secretly __5__ many people to freedom in the North. One of its conductors was Harriet Tubman, who was never __6__ about speaking out against slavery. __7__ who bought Harriet Beecher Stowe's novel *Uncle Tom's Cabin* joined in supporting the antislavery movement. Once in the North, some former slaves were helped by the __8__ of those supporters until they found work. Although far from a(n) __9__ way to settle differences, the Civil War taught us that freedom was a(n) __10__ right many Americans once took for granted.

1. _____

2. _____

3. _____

4. _____

5. _____

6. _____

7. _____

8. _____

9. _____

10. _____

Word Learning—Group B

Study the spelling, part(s) of speech, and meaning(s) of each word from Group B. Complete each sentence by writing the word on the line. Then read the sentence.

1. **allegiance** *(n.)* faithfulness or loyalty to someone or something

   It is easy to have _____ to a basketball team that always wins.

2. **chemical** *(n.)* a substance that may be combined with others to create new substances

   Carefully measure out the _____ and pour it into a test tube.

3. **climate** *(n.)* the kind of weather a place has; environment

   I prefer a warm _____ where I can swim outside all year.

4. **equator** *(n.)* an imaginary circle around the middle of the earth

   The continent of Australia is south of the _____.

5. **galaxy** *(n.)* a collection of billions of stars

   The astronomer spied a distant _____ through her telescope.

6. **geography** *(n.)* the study of the earth's surface, climate, people, continents, and products

   To know more about earthquakes and where they happen, take a

   class on world _____.

7. **horizon** *(n.)* where the earth and sky seem to meet

   The cruise ship seemed to slip over the _____ and into the setting sun.

8. **invisible** *(adj.)* not visible; not able to be seen

   Bacteria may be _____, but they can cause visible changes to the world around us.

9. **prey** *(n.)* an animal hunted for food

   The nature film featured a lion chasing its _____.

10. reflect *(v.)* 1. to give back or throw back light, heat, or sound; 2. to send back an image or a likeness

The spy held up a mirror to _____ the light back into the guard's eyes.

Use Your Vocabulary—Group B

Choose the word from Group B that best completes each sentence. Write the word on the line. You may use the plural form of nouns and the past tense of verbs if necessary.

I flew across the __1__ as I traveled above South America. I was headed to tropical Peru, where the __2__ is warm all year. I studied the __3__ of Peru before my trip and found that it has many rivers and mountains. From one of those mountaintops, I watched a beautiful sunset melt into the __4__. Then I gazed at what appeared to be an entire __5__ of stars and wondered what __6__ reactions could make the stars appear so bright. I heard an animal prowling nearby, probably in search of its __7__. The next day I marveled at the bright sun __8__ in the glass buildings of the city of Lima. I talked with many people who were unhappy with the government. Others said that their __9__ lay with their government. When it was time to leave, my jet climbed above the clouds and the now __10__ city became just a pleasant memory.

1. _____

2. _____

3. _____

4. _____

5. _____

6. _____

7. _____

8. _____

9. _____

10. _____

Notable Quotes

"The fluttering of a butterfly's wings can effect **climate** changes on the other side of the planet."

Paul R. Ehrlich (1932–), entomologist

SYNONYMS

Synonyms are words that have the same or nearly the same meanings.

Part 1 Choose the word from the box that is the best synonym for each group of words. Write the word on the line.

charity	horizon	precious	reflect	consumer
prey	bashful	climate	relish	chemical

1. border, limit, edge _____

2. costly, dear, valuable _____

3. substance, compound _____

4. compassion, kindness _____

5. echo, mirror, throw back _____

6. victim, game, quarry _____

7. retiring, timid, humble _____

8. flavoring, seasoning; enjoy _____

9. customer, shopper, buyer _____

10. characteristic weather _____

Vocabulary in Action

The **equator** is a line around the earth. It divides the earth into the Northern and Southern Hemispheres. It crosses the continents of South America and Africa as well as many islands in the Indian and Pacific Oceans. In most parts of the world, the number of hours of daytime and nighttime changes with the seasons. In places along the equator, daytime and nighttime are always 12 hours long. In fact, the word *equator* comes from a phrase that means "circle equalizing day and night."

Part 2 Replace the underlined word(s) with a word from the box that means the same or almost the same. Write your answer on the line.

liberty	transport	geography	galaxy	formless
satisfactory	allegiance	invisible	equator	luxury

11. The workers were asked for their complete <u>devotion</u> to the company.

_____

12. Our solar system is a very small part of a large <u>star cluster</u>.

_____

13. Julia's old car may not be fast, but it provides <u>adequate</u> transportation.

_____

14. We will need a very large truck to <u>move</u> everything at once.

_____

15. As the fog rolled in, the airport was <u>out of sight</u> to the incoming planes. _____

16. The revolutionary soldiers demanded <u>freedom</u> for their captured comrades. _____

17. Next year's clothing fashions will feature a <u>shapeless</u> sort of dress.

_____

18. Some expensive hotels provide the <u>special pleasure</u> of fresh flowers in each room. _____

19. Somewhere in Africa, tourists can stand with one foot on each side of the <u>imaginary line that divides the earth</u>. _____

20. My new atlas has maps that show the <u>land formations</u> of each country. _____

 **ANTONYMS**

Antonyms are words that have opposite or nearly opposite meanings.

Part 1 Choose the word from the box that is the best antonym for each group of words. Write the word on the line.

luxury	allegiance	invisible
reflect	liberty	formless

1. slavery, dependence, captivity   _____

2. absorb, take in   _____

3. shaped, geometric, rigid   _____

4. basic, necessity, requirement   _____

5. disloyalty, treason, betrayal   _____

6. seen, obvious, in view   _____

Part 2 Replace the underlined word with a word from the box that means the opposite or almost the opposite. Write your answer on the line.

precious	charity	consumer
bashful	relish	satisfactory

7. The young man entered the office in a <u>bold</u> manner.

_____

8. As a <u>producer</u> of baked goods, he found he had trouble losing weight.

_____

9. Makayla and Molly <u>dislike</u> the idea of getting up early each morning for band practice. _____

10. Some said the ballplayer appeared merely for the publicity; others called it an act of <u>greed</u>. _____

11. Trevor's power tools are <u>useless</u> for this job. _____

12. Grandmother's old furniture is <u>worthless</u> to me. _____

WORD STUDY

Homophones Write the homophones from the box below on the lines to complete what each person said.

> piece   peace   waste   waist   aisle   isle

1. The bride said, "After I walk down the church _____ with my groom, we will honeymoon on a small Caribbean _____."

2. The party guest said, "I don't want to _____ any of my dinner, but if I eat all of this, I won't be able to button my jacket around my _____."

3. The pastry chef said, "I won't get any _____ around here until I give each customer a(n) _____ of my famous apple pie."

CHALLENGE WORDS

Word Learning–Challenge!

Study the spelling, part(s) of speech, and meaning(s) of each word below. Complete each sentence by writing the word on the line. Then read the sentence.

1. **aroma** *(n.)* a fragrance

   The _____ of baking bread makes my mouth water.

2. **deface** *(v.)* to damage; to spoil the appearance of

   If you _____ this door with spray paint, you'll be punished.

3. **dismantle** *(v.)* 1. to pull down; 2. to take something apart

   We must _____ the dollhouse and put the pieces away.

4. enlighten *(v.)* 1. to make clear; 2. to inform; 3. to instruct

Please _____ me of your whereabouts.

5. obstinate *(adj.)* stubborn; not giving in

This _____ mule refuses to move from the middle of the road.

Use Your Vocabulary—Challenge!

Eyewitness to History Choose a time in history when a war was fought. Imagine that you are there shortly after an important battle. On a separate sheet of paper, write an eyewitness account of the scene. Use the Challenge Words below. Be sure the reader knows which time in history you chose.

| aroma | deface | dismantle | enlighten | obstinate |

FUN WITH WORDS

Unscramble the vocabulary words in each group. Write the words in the blanks. Then draw a line from each unscrambled word to its definition.

Group 1

1. uuxrly   _____   • an animal hunted for food

2. blisivine   _____   • beyond what is necessary

3. zoniroh   _____   • not able to be seen

4. calimech   _____   • a substance that may be combined with others to create new substances

5. rype   _____   • where the earth and sky seem to meet

Group 2

1. tlecfre   _____

2. quetroa   _____

3. ctialme   _____

4. lyxaga   _____

5. phragyoge   _____

- an imaginary circle around the middle of the earth
- a collection of billions of stars forming one system
- study of the earth's land, climate, people, and products
- to send back an image
- the kind of weather a place has

Group 3

1. liglencaae   _____

2. sprtaotnr   _____

3. eishlr   _____

4. soncumre   _____

5. flubash   _____

- to carry from one place to another
- faithfulness or loyalty to someone or something
- uneasy around others
- a buyer and a user of goods and services
- to like the taste of

Group 4

1. aiaorytfsstc   _____

2. yrthaic   _____

3. trebily   _____

4. slemfors   _____

5. suoicerp   _____

- good enough to fulfill desires, hopes, and demands
- of great value
- a generous giving to those who are poor, sick, or helpless
- the right or power to do as one pleases
- having no regular shape

CHAPTER 4

WORD LIST

Read each word using the pronunciation key.

Group A

capacity (kə pas´ ə tē)
compare (kəm pâr´)
decision (di sizh´ ən)
difference (dif´ ər əns)
forbid (fər bid´)
impatient (im pā´ shənt)
objection (ob jek´ shən)
reflection (ri flek´ shən)
reorganize (rē ôr´ gə nīz)
scarce (skârs)

Group B

ancestor (an´ ses tər)
citizen (sit´ ə zən)
companion (kəm pan´ yən)
manufacturer (man yə fak´ chər ər)
merchant (mər´ chənt)
minister (min´ is tər)
orphan (ôr´ fən)
professional (prə fesh´ ən əl)
surgeon (sər´ jən)
usher (ush´ ər)

WORD STUDY

Analogies

An analogy is a comparison between different things. Read and study the following analogies.

Yellow is to **lemon** as **green** is to **celery.**

Ink is to **pen** as **paint** is to **brush.**

Bee is to **hive** as **bird** is to **nest.**

Challenge Words

alter (ôl´ tər)
bisect (bī´ sekt)
boycott (boi´ kot)
curtail (kər tāl´)
sequel (sē´ kwəl)

Read each sentence below to figure out the meaning of the word in **bold**. Use reasoning skills and the remainder of the sentence to help you. Write the meaning of the word on the line.

1. The clothing **merchant** on Wolcott Street sold me this wool coat.

_____

2. You will have trouble finding what you want because ripe tomatoes are **scarce** in winter.

_____

3. The young kitten was an **orphan** after its mother ran away.

_____

4. My mother said it was time to **reorganize** my closet, which was stuffed with piles of clothes and toys.

_____

5. As we hiked past Crater Lake, I saw our **reflection** in the water.

_____

6. The woman explained that her little dog is her **companion** and goes with her everywhere.

_____

7. The **usher** said, "Watch your step" as he showed me to my seat.

_____

8. As we looked at old photographs of our family, my father told me about our **ancestor** from Japan.

_____

9. The **impatient** man honked his car horn and yelled, "Get moving!"

_____

10. My sister and her fiancé met with a **minister** to pick a wedding date.

_____

WORD MEANINGS

Word Learning—Group A

Study the spelling, part(s) of speech, and meaning(s) of each word from Group A. Complete each sentence by writing the word on the line. Then read the sentence.

1. **capacity** *(n.)* the largest amount something can hold

   The bucket is filled to _____ and is spilling over.

2. **compare** *(v.)* to note what is alike and what is different

   I was asked to _____ three spaghetti sauces and choose the best one.

3. **decision** *(n.)* a judgment reached

   Listen to both sides of an argument before you make a

   _____.

4. **difference** *(n.)* characteristic that distinguishes one thing from another

   Even though both vases were made by the same person, there is a great

   _____ between them.

5. **forbid** *(v.)* 1. to not allow; 2. to make a rule against

   Christopher's parents _____ him to go to a movie on a school night.

6. **impatient** *(adj.)* 1. not willing to wait or bear delay; 2. short of temper due to irritation

   Waiting for the movie to start, the children were _____.

7. **objection** *(n.)* 1. disapproval of something; 2. argument against something

   The mayor raised an _____ to the reporter's question.

8. **reflection** *(n.)* 1. the throwing back of rays; 2. image or likeness

   She glanced at her _____ in the mirror.

9. reorganize *(v.)* 1. to organize or form again; 2. to arrange in a new way

I need to _____ my locker so that I can find my books more quickly.

10. scarce *(adj.)* hard to find or get; rare

The geologist finally found the _____ minerals.

Use Your Vocabulary—Group A

Choose the word from Group A that best completes each sentence. Write the word on the line. You may use the plural form of nouns and the past tense of verbs if necessary.

Doctor Daedelus said, "Fill the beaker to **1** with the bubbling potion."

"No," his patient, Ichabod, replied. "I **2** you to do any more painful experiments on me."

"Look at your **3** in this mirror," Doctor Daedelus said. " **4** your new looks to this old photograph of you. Can't you see how much better you look?"

"The only **5** I see," Ichabod said, "is in my hair."

"But, Ichabod, little by little the experiment will **6** your facial features," Doctor Daedelus said. "In fact, this photo has helped me make a(n) **7** . Let's move your eyebrows closer to your ears!"

"No, Doctor," Ichabod protested. "I must raise a(n) **8** . My eyebrows are just fine where they are."

"Careful, Ichabod! Do not spill any of the potion from the beaker. It is **9** , and I may not be able to get more."

In a(n) **10** voice, Ichabod exclaimed, "Oh, Doctor! I've had enough of your foolish work! I quit!"

1. _____

2. _____

3. _____

4. _____

5. _____

6. _____

7. _____

8. _____

9. _____

10. _____

Word Learning—Group B

Study the spelling, part(s) of speech, and meaning(s) of each word from Group B. Complete each sentence by writing the word on the line. Then read the sentence.

1. ancestor *(n.)* relative who lived a long time ago

I was amazed to learn that my _____ was a queen.

2. citizen *(n.)* member of a nation

Pierre, our foreign-exchange student, is a _____ of France.

3. companion *(n.)* one who spends time with another

Ashley is my _____ on long walks through the woods.

4. manufacturer *(n.)* a person or company whose business is to make something by hand or machine

Haley's company is a _____ of stuffed animals.

5. merchant *(n.)* a person who buys or sells goods for a living; *(adj.)* trading

The jewelry _____ is offering a discount on gold earrings.

These _____ ships once transported spices.

6. minister *(n.)* a member of the clergy serving in a church; *(v.)* to work and care for

The congregation followed the _____ into the church.

Hospital chaplains _____ to those who are sick.

7. orphan *(n.)* 1. a child whose parents are no longer living; 2. a young animal without a mother

Thomas became an _____ at the age of 16.

8. professional *(n.)* an expert in a particular field, such as law, medicine, or teaching; *(adj.)* having something to do with a job requiring special education

Don't try to paint the car yourself; call a _____.

The architect gave us her _____ opinion.

9. surgeon *(n.)* doctor who performs operations

They were called in to discuss the operation with the

_____.

10. usher *(n.)* one who leads people to their seats in a church or public hall; *(v.)* to show the way to

She took the arm of the _____ and walked into the theater.

"Who will _____ me to my box seat?" asked the movie critic.

Use Your Vocabulary—Group B

Choose the word from Group B that best completes each sentence. Write the word on the line. You may use the plural form of nouns and the past tense of verbs if necessary.

I recently traced my family tree because I plan to write a book about my __1__. To begin the search, my traveling __2__ and I went to Chicago, New York, and London to look at documents about my family. I found that many of my relatives were __3__ with jobs in medicine, such as my great-grandfather who was a well-known heart __4__. My great-uncle, a fur __5__, lost his store in the great Chicago Fire of 1871. After the fire, he opened a factory and became a(n) __6__ of fire hoses. Another relative worked as a(n) __7__ at the famous Radio City Music Hall in New York City. One of my second cousins became a(n) __8__ when her parents died in the World War II bombing of London. She then moved to New York to live with the family of a __9__. After a few years in the United States, she gave up her ties to England and became a U.S. __10__.

1. _____

2. _____

3. _____

4. _____

5. _____

6. _____

7. _____

8. _____

9. _____

10. _____

SYNONYMS

Synonyms are words that have the same or nearly the same meanings.

Part 1 Choose the word from the box that is the best synonym for each group of words. Write the word on the line.

scarce	surgeon	citizen	orphan	capacity
professional	reflection	usher	companion	compare

1. doctor, specialist   _____

2. rare, uncommon   _____

3. relate, liken, match   _____

4. friend, mate, partner   _____

5. member of a state, national   _____

6. limit, volume, size   _____

7. expert, specially trained person   _____

8. guide, escort; lead, conduct   _____

9. copy, image, echo   _____

10. parentless child, foundling   _____

Vocabulary in Action

The word **companion** comes to us from Latin. The first part of the word, *com,* means "with." The second part comes from the Latin *panis,* which means "bread." So the word *companion* could be said to mean "with bread" or "bread buddy." This refers to the fact that someone you shared bread with was probably a friend or companion. The word first appeared in the English language at the end of the 13th century or the beginning of the 14th century.

Part 2 Replace the underlined word with a word from the box that means the same or almost the same. Write your answer on the line.

objection	forbid	decision	impatient	difference
merchant	ancestors	reorganize	manufacturer	minister

11. Kilkenny Castle was the ancient home of Mr. Butler's <u>forebears</u>.

_____

12. The <u>judgment</u> of the football referees will be final. _____

13. The <u>contrast</u> between the students amazes me. _____

14. Waiting for the play to begin, Paige was so <u>restless</u> that she could

hardly sit in her seat. _____

15. The police will <u>prevent</u> reporters from entering the crime scene.

_____

16. The <u>storekeeper</u> offered a summer job to anyone who wanted to sell

ice cream. _____

17. Mr. Smith made his fortune as a <u>maker</u> of steel. _____

18. The <u>preacher</u> will speak after the choir sings. _____

19. Is there any <u>argument</u> you would like to present to the student council?

_____

20. Students will <u>rearrange</u> all the library books. _____

Notable Quotes

"There is no king who has not had a slave among his
ancestors, and no slave who has not had a king among his."

—Helen Keller (1880–1968), author, activist

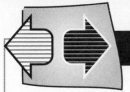

ANTONYMS

Antonyms are words that have opposite or nearly opposite meanings.

Part 1 Choose the word from the box that is the best antonym for each group of words. Write the word on the line.

| forbid | decision | difference | objection | ancestor |

1. children, descendant, offspring _____

2. encourage, approve _____

3. agreement, approval _____

4. unity, likeness, similarity _____

5. no opinion, hesitation _____

Part 2 Replace the underlined word with a word from the box that means the opposite or almost the opposite. Write your answer on the line.

| scarce | citizens | professional | impatient |

6. Our coach gets <u>calm</u> whenever the team falls behind.

_____

7. All <u>visitors</u> are expected to follow the laws of this country.

_____

8. The weather is responsible for the <u>plentiful</u> crop this spring.

_____

9. The new TV channel broadcasts <u>amateur</u> sports. _____

Vocabulary in Action

The prefix *im-* is a variation of *in-*, which means "not." Therefore, *impatient* means "not patient." Other variations of *in-* include *il-* and *ir-*.

WORD STUDY

Analogies Complete each analogy with a word from the box.

| merchant | minister | forbid | ancestor | surgeon |

1. **School** is to **principal** as **church** is to _____.

2. **Athlete** is to **football player** as **doctor** is to _____.

3. **Patient** is to **dentist** as **customer** is to _____.

4. **Permit** is to **allow** as **prevent** is to _____.

5. **Father** is to **parent** as **great-grandfather** is to _____.

CHALLENGE WORDS

Word Learning—Challenge!

Study the spelling, part(s) of speech, and meaning(s) of each word. Complete each sentence by writing the word on the line. Then read the sentence.

1. **alter** *(v.)* to make or become different; to change

   I need to _____ these pants to make them shorter.

2. **bisect** *(v.)* to divide into two usually equal parts

   You can _____ a 30-degree angle into two 15-degree angles.

3. **boycott** *(v.)* to join together and refuse to buy from or associate with; *(n.)* the act of boycotting

   We will _____ this store because they pay low wages.

   Our _____ of the store ended when the owners agreed to pay their workers more money.

4. **curtail** *(v.)* 1. to cut short; 2. to stop part of

   We had to _____ the game and go home early because of rain.

5. sequel *(n.)* a complete story continuing an earlier one with the same characters

The _____ to the movie was even better than the first!

Use Your Vocabulary—Challenge!

The New Relative You discover a long-lost relative who once led a boycott. This relative also writes books and draws floor plans for houses. Imagine that you interview this fascinating person. On a separate sheet of paper, write your interview using the Challenge Words below. Be sure to tell who the relative is and where and when the interview took place.

alter	bisect	boycott	curtail	sequel

FUN WITH WORDS

Use the clues to complete the puzzle on page 54. Choose from the words in the box.

capacity	decision	merchant	reorganize
companion	forbid	minister	scarce
compare	manufacturer	orphan	surgeon

Across

1. person who buys or sells goods for a living
2. one who goes with another
3. hard to find
6. child whose parents are no longer living
8. largest amount something can hold
9. to arrange in a new way
10. doctor who performs operations
11. to not allow

Down

1. person whose business is to make something by hand or machine
4. to note what is alike and what is different among
5. a judgment reached
7. to be of service; to work and care for

Notable Quotes

"An individual's self-concept is the core of his personality. It affects every aspect of human behavior: the ability to learn, the **capacity** to grow and change."

—Dr. Joyce Brothers (1928–), psychologist, advice columnist

Review 3–4

WORD MEANINGS

Fill in the bubble of the word that is best defined by each phrase.

1. easily embarrassed
   - (a.) impatient
   - (b.) bashful
   - (c.) precious
   - (d.) invisible

2. weather in a particular place
   - (a.) liberty
   - (b.) capacity
   - (c.) climate
   - (d.) citizen

3. giving to those who are poor, ill, or otherwise in need
   - (a.) charity
   - (b.) luxury
   - (c.) objection
   - (d.) merchant

4. worth a great deal
   - (a.) formless
   - (b.) impatient
   - (c.) bashful
   - (d.) precious

5. a devotion to someone or something
   - (a.) allegiance
   - (b.) reflection
   - (c.) decision
   - (d.) geography

6. to make a rule that does not allow
   - (a.) compare
   - (b.) forbid
   - (c.) minister
   - (d.) relish

7. one who buys and uses goods and services
   - (a.) ancestor
   - (b.) consumer
   - (c.) surgeon
   - (d.) orphan

8. to throw back light
   - (a.) reflect
   - (b.) transport
   - (c.) relish
   - (d.) reorganize

9. an expert in a particular job
   - (a.) companion
   - (b.) galaxy
   - (c.) consumer
   - (d.) professional

10. one who makes things for a living
    - (a.) consumer
    - (b.) prey
    - (c.) manufacturer
    - (d.) surgeon

11. not willing to put up with something
    - (a.) impatient
    - (b.) formless
    - (c.) professional
    - (d.) invisible

12. the amount something can hold when full
    - (a.) charity
    - (b.) capacity
    - (c.) luxury
    - (d.) decision

13. to arrange again
    - (a.) transport
    - (b.) forbid
    - (c.) reorganize
    - (d.) reflect

14. something that flavors food
    - (a.) luxury
    - (b.) prey
    - (c.) horizon
    - (d.) relish

15. one who guides
    - (a.) merchant
    - (b.) usher
    - (c.) companion
    - (d.) citizen

SENTENCE COMPLETION

Choose the word from Part 1 that best completes each of the following sentences. Write the word in the blank. Then do the same for Part 2. You will not use all the words.

Part 1

citizen	surgeon	equator	horizon
merchant	companion	scarce	liberty

1. When I became a(n) _____ of this country, I pledged my loyalty to the United States.

2. The _____ is an imaginary line around the center of the earth.

3. We tried to find a black one, but the supply was _____.

4. A(n) _____ must always scrub his or her hands and put on gloves before performing an operation.

5. My twin sister is my constant _____. We do everything together.

Part 2

transports	formless	prey	chemical
galaxy	satisfactory	decision	compares

6. I received a(n) _____ grade in Spanish after completing my final exam.

7. My cat's favorite _____ are mice from the fields behind our house.

8. My friend the truck driver _____ goods from Georgia all the way to Alaska.

9. Do not use that _____ to clean with; it is dangerous!

10. Luke finally made a(n) _____ and ordered the silver one.

CHAPTER 5

WORD LIST

Read each word using the pronunciation key.

Group A

batch (bach)
desirable (di zī´ rə bəl)
flexible (flek´ sə bəl)
forecast (fôr´ kast)
gauge (gāj)
gland (gland)
paralyze (pâr´ ə līz)
plateau (pla tō´)
vapor (vā´ pər)
whine (wīn)

Group B

bacteria (bak tir´ ē ə)
banquet (bāŋ´ kwit)
defrost (di frost´)
dispute (di spyo͞ot´)
dungeon (dun´ jən)
easel (ē´ zəl)
foreign (fôr´ in)
foundation (foun dā´ shən)
museum (myo͞o zē´ əm)
operation (op ə rā´ shən)

WORD STUDY

Suffixes

The suffix -ward means "in the direction of."

skyward (skī´ wərd) *(adv.)* toward the sky
backward (bak´ wərd) *(adv.)* toward the back
homeward (hōm´ wərd) *(adv.)* toward home
upward (up´ wərd) *(adv.)* toward a higher place
downward (doun´ wərd) *(adv.)* toward a lower place
westward (west´ wərd) *(adv.)* toward the west

Challenge Words

economical (e kə nom´ i kəl)
fathom (fath´ əm)
morose (mə rōs´)
perjure (pər´ jər)
refuge (ref´ yo͞oj)

Read each sentence below to figure out the meaning of the word in **bold**. Use reasoning skills and the remainder of the sentence to help you. Write the meaning of the word on the line.

1. Lauren was able to **defrost** her frozen dinner in the microwave oven.

_____

2. The scientists observed **bacteria** under a high-powered microscope.

_____

3. From where they were standing on the **plateau**, the explorers could see the land for miles.

_____

4. Daniel used a tape measure to **gauge** the distance between the bases on the field.

_____

5. The **museum** was fun to visit and a great place to learn more about history.

_____

6. Once he returned to the United States, Hunter discovered that he couldn't buy anything with the **foreign** money left in his pocket.

_____

7. Juan made a **batch** of oatmeal cookies for the neighborhood picnic.

_____

8. The living conditions in the deep, dark **dungeon** were terrible, but the prisoner had no chance to escape.

_____

9. Because so many people came to the **banquet**, the chefs ran out of food.

_____

10. We can settle this height **dispute** if Natalie would stand up straight.

_____

WORD MEANINGS

Word Learning—Group A

Study the spelling, part(s) of speech, and meaning(s) of each word from Group A. Complete each sentence by writing the word on the line. Then read the sentence.

1. batch *(n.)* a quantity of something made at one time

Let's buy flour, butter, sugar, and chocolate chips and make a

_____ of cookies.

2. desirable *(adj.)* 1. worth wanting or doing; 2. worth having; 3. pleasing

For a fan of the newest video games, a high-powered computer is most

_____.

3. flexible *(adj.)* bendable; not stiff

My _____ fishing rod bent with the weight of the big fish.

4. forecast *(v.)* to predict or tell beforehand

What do they _____ for tomorrow's weather?

5. gauge *(v.)* 1. to measure precisely; 2. to estimate; *(n.)* an instrument for measuring or testing

A good driver will _____ a safe distance between his or her car and the car in front.

The gas _____ reads nearly empty on my mom's car.

6. gland *(n.)* a body organ that makes and gives out some substance

Just the thought of chocolate cream pie makes my salivary

_____ work overtime.

7. paralyze *(v.)* 1. to make helpless or unable to move; 2. to stun

This drug will _____ the gorilla long enough so the vet can pull his bad tooth.

8. plateau *(n.)* a large area of level, high ground

Brad and Nicolas climbed to the level ground of the _____.

9. vapor *(n.)* 1. any moisture in the air that can be seen; 2. steam, mist, or fog

A machine used on movie sets creates water _____ for an eerie atmosphere.

10. whine *(v.)* to complain in a childish and annoying way; *(n.)* a long, high-pitched sound

If you _____ about getting your dessert once more, there will be none served.

The steady _____ of the jet engines made talking impossible.

Use Your Vocabulary—Group A

Choose the word from Group A that best completes each sentence. Write the word on the line. You may use the plural form of nouns and the past tense of verbs if necessary.

Kaylee put the bag with the the last __1__ of cookies into her backpack and called to her mom, "We better hurry if we want to hike to the top of the __2__ and back before sunset." Her mom came in and said, "The weather report __3__ rain today. Do you still want to go?" Kaylee __4__ the situation as she felt the __5__ in her neck, and said, "My throat is a little sore, but I won't __6__. Let's go." __7__ hung over the valley as Kaylee's mom drove in the predawn hours. Suddenly, a deer leapt into the road and seemed __8__ by the headlights before it ran away. "It is really pretty at this time," Kaylee's mom said. "I'm glad you were __9__ and decided to go." Kaylee said, "I am too. This is much more __10__ than just watching TV."

1. _____

2. _____

3. _____

4. _____

5. _____

6. _____

7. _____

8. _____

9. _____

10. _____

Word Learning—Group B

Study the spelling, part(s) of speech, and meaning(s) of each word from Group B. Complete each sentence by writing the word on the line. Then read the sentence.

1. **bacteria** *(n.)* tiny, living things that can be seen only through a microscope

   Sickness can be spread by _____ on unwashed hands.

2. **banquet** *(n.)* 1. a big, formal meal; 2. a feast

   When Mrs. Deal retired after 50 years of service, the company held a _____ in her honor.

3. **defrost** *(v.)* 1. to remove ice or frost from; 2. to thaw

   A few days before Thanksgiving is a good time to _____ the frozen turkey.

4. **dispute** *(v.)* 1. to argue or discuss; 2. to debate; *(n.)* a quarrel

   I will _____ your idea that it's my turn to dust.

   Erik and Zoe flipped a coin to settle their _____ over who will clean the bathroom.

5. **dungeon** *(n.)* a dark, underground prison cell

   As part of the castle tour, we inched down narrow steps to see the

   _____.

6. **easel** *(n.)* a stand for displaying or holding a picture

   The painter displayed his finished painting on the wooden

   _____.

7. **foreign** *(adj.)* of, from, or typical of another part of the world

   Martin needs a passport to leave the United States and travel to

   _____ countries.

8. **foundation** *(n.)* the base on which something stands

   The workers need to first lay bricks to make the _____ for the new house.

9. museum *(n.)* a building in which a collection of objects is kept and displayed

This _____ has paintings from around the world.

10. operation *(n.)* the way something works

The detailed pictures of the inside helped me understand the

_____ of a toaster.

Use Your Vocabulary—Group B

Choose the word from Group B that best completes each sentence. Write the word on the line. You may use the plural form of nouns and the past tense of verbs if necessary.

When our class went to an art __1__, the tour started on the dark lower level of the huge stone building. It felt a bit like a deep, dark __2__. Inside the galleries, though, bright lights shone on colorful paintings. There were paintings and sculptures by American and __3__ artists. I liked the one that showed a lot of people feasting at a huge __4__. Two others showed a scientist looking at __5__ under a microscope and an artist painting a picture at his __6__. Another showed a sagging building whose brick __7__ was crumbling. One painting of a snowstorm made me feel so cold that I said I needed to go somewhere warm to __8__. Another painting showed doctors performing a brain __9__. I thought it was great, but my friends __10__ me. They didn't like the painting at all.

1. _____

2. _____

3. _____

4. _____

5. _____

6. _____

7. _____

8. _____

9. _____

10. _____

Notable Quotes

"The first rule of any technology used in a business is that automation applied to an efficient **operation** will magnify the efficiency. The second is that automation applied to an inefficient operation will magnify the inefficiency."

—Bill Gates (1955–), co-founder of Microsoft, philanthropist

SYNONYMS

Synonyms are words that have the same or nearly the same meanings.

Part 1 Choose the word from the box that is the best synonym for each group of words. Write the word on the line.

| operation | foreign | defrost | whine | flexible |
| batch | forecast | banquet | dispute | plateau |

1. from another land, alien, exotic _____

2. whimper, gripe; a wail, moan _____

3. elastic, easily bent _____

4. group, bunch, amount _____

5. large dinner, elegant meal _____

6. challenge, question; an argument _____

7. procedure, performance, activity _____

8. melt, warm _____

9. foresee, envision, calculate _____

10. mesa, highland, upland _____

Vocabulary in Action

Our word ***museum*** can be traced back to the Greek word *Mouseion*. This Greek word meant "shrine of the Muses." In Greek mythology the Muses were nine daughters of the god Zeus. Each of the Muses was the guardian of a different kind of art or science. Many artists and writers thought that the inspiration for the greatest works came from the Muses. Today, we still call something that inspires our creativity a muse.

Part 2 Replace the underlined word(s) with a word from the box that means the same or almost the same. Write your answer on the line.

paralyze	bacteria	museum	foundation	vapor
desirable	glands	gauge	dungeon	easel

11. The headlights of the car seemed to <u>freeze</u> the raccoon as it was crossing the road. _____

12. When the guilty prisoner is sentenced, he will be taken to the <u>underground cell</u>. _____

13. To excel at math, you need a good knowledge <u>base</u> of fundamental facts. _____

14. The advertising agency will <u>judge</u> the success of its ads by asking you questions about the product. _____

15. Getting a ride to school on a rainy day would be <u>advantageous</u>.

    _____

16. We watched <u>fog</u> roll in off the lake this morning. _____

17. This mouthwash claims to kill the <u>germs</u> that cause bad breath.

    _____

18. The room had a wooden <u>art stand</u> with finger paints for each budding artist. _____

19. We lingered in the <u>showroom</u> of antique cars called "Streets of Yesterday." _____

20. If the <u>organs</u> under your jaw are swollen, it could mean that you are ill. _____

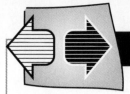

ANTONYMS

Antonyms are words that have opposite or nearly opposite meanings.

Part 1 Choose the word from the box that is the antonym for each group of words. Write the word on the line.

dungeon	dispute	whine
paralyze	foreign	batch

1. agree with; an agreement _____

2. cause to move, make powerful _____

3. one, a single unit, sole _____

4. low, quiet humming noise _____

5. place of freedom _____

6. domestic, native, of one's country _____

Part 2 Replace the underlined word with a word from the box that means the opposite or almost the opposite. Write your answer on the line.

foundation	plateau	desirable
defrost	flexible	banquet

7. There's a view of the mountains from this <u>valley</u>. _____

8. We celebrated the end of the football season with a <u>snack</u> in the school cafeteria. _____

9. Mom is usually very <u>firm</u> in her curfew hours. _____

10. As Ruben read the menu, he thought the asparagus with cheese was <u>unappealing</u>. _____

11. Take the package of vegetables out of the grocery bag and <u>freeze</u> it.

_____

12. The earthquake did no damage to the walls, but the <u>roof</u> is cracked.

_____

WORD STUDY

Suffixes Use the words in the box below to answer the questions.

skyward	backward	homeward
upward	downward	westward

1. What two words in the box are opposites?

_____ _____

2. How would you describe the path of rockets, airplanes, and birds?

_____

3. Which direction is opposite of going east? _____

4. Where are you likely to travel at the end of the day?

_____

5. When you count from 10 to 1, in which direction are you counting?

_____

CHALLENGE WORDS

Word Learning—Challenge!

Study the spelling, part(s) of speech, and meaning(s) of each word.
Complete each sentence by writing the word on the line. Then read
the sentence.

1. economical *(adj.)* avoiding waste; efficient; saving

This family-size box of cereal is more _____ than the
small size.

2. **fathom** *(n.)* a unit of length equal to six feet, used to measure the depth of water

The diver swam down one _____ to the coral reefs.

3. **morose** *(adj.)* gloomy; sullen; glum

On days when I'm feeling _____, I like to cheer myself up with a funny movie.

4. **perjure** *(v.)* to cause the voluntary violation of an oath; to swear falsely

If you tell a lie in court and _____ yourself, you will be punished.

5. **refuge** *(n.)* shelter or protection from danger or difficulty

An overhanging roof makes a good _____ from the rain.

Use Your Vocabulary—Challenge!

Sub Thieves Imagine that you have seen a new movie about a gang of thieves who are caught trying to steal a submarine. On a separate sheet of paper, write a review of this movie using the Challenge Words below. Be sure to tell what the title is, what happens in the story, and what you think of the movie.

economical   fathom   morose   perjure   refuge

FUN WITH WORDS

An anagram is a word made by mixing up the letters of one word in order to spell another word. For instance, rearranging the letters of the word *moat* gives us the anagram *atom*. The letters are the same; they're just in a different order.

In the game below, you'll see an equation like this:

undone + g = a place you don't want to be _____

The letters to the left of the equal sign are an anagram of one of the words from this chapter (plus one or two additional letters that are needed to complete the vocabulary word). The words to the right of the equal sign give you a hint. In the sample above, combine the letters from the word *undone* with the letter *g* and rearrange them. You should come up with *dungeon*, which is definitely a place you don't want to be! Write the vocabulary word in the blank provided, and you're done with that equation. Now try to untangle the anagrams below.

1. glad + n = something everybody has   _____

2. rap + vo = it's in the air   _____

3. side + put = people taking opposite sides   _____

4. leap + uta = don't leap from here   _____

5. win + he = even if you don't win,
   don't do this   _____

6. store + df = an anagram that needs
   to warm up   _____

7. painter + oo = how does this work?   _____

8. belief + xl = a highly bendable word   _____

9. replay + az = don't freeze up!   _____

10. beadier + ls = you want these beads   _____

11. craft + soe = it's a craft to get this right   _____

12. hat + cb = not one hat but several   _____

13. seal + e = you won't see a seal use this   _____

14. grin + foe = give a grin to someone
   who is this   _____

15. tribe + aca = a tribe of these is tiny   _____

WORD LIST

Read each word using the pronunciation key.

Group A

accuse (ə kyōōz´)
compass (kum´ pəs)
complain (kəm plān´)
disappoint (dis ə point´)
exaggerate (ig zaj´ ə rāt)
independence (in di pen´ dəns)
masquerade (mas kə rād´)
melody (mel´ ə dē)
sanitary (san´ i ter ē)
vacant (vā´ kənt)

Group B

campaign (kam pān´)
disarrange (dis ə rānj´)
echo (ek´ ō)
fault (fôlt)
fraction (frak´ shən)
haste (hāst)
horrid (hôr´ id)
justice (jus´ tis)
latitude (lat´ i tōōd)
magnetize (mag´ ni tīz)

WORD STUDY

Prefixes

The prefix *re-* means "again."

react (rē akt´) *(v.)* to act back
replace (rē plās´) *(v.)* to fill or take the place of
recall (rē kol´) *(v.)* to call back to mind; to remember
rebuild (rē bild´) *(v.)* to build again
reuse (rē yōōz´) *(v.)* to use again

Challenge Words

compose (kəm pōs´)
inaugurate (in ô´ gyə rāt)
pallor (pal´ ər)
periodical (pir ē od´ ə kəl)
relent (ri lent´)

WORDS IN CONTEXT

Read each sentence below to figure out the meaning of the word in **bold**. Use reasoning skills and the remainder of the sentence to help you. Write the meaning of the word on the line.

1. Brandy wants to **masquerade** as a vendor to get into the sold-out game.

   _____

2. The song's **melody** reminded Kayla of a tune her dad used to whistle.

   _____

3. Brittney forgot to set her alarm, so it was her own **fault** that she was late for swimming practice.

   _____

4. Ethan has no reason to **accuse** me of putting worms in his lunch box, but he still thinks I did it.

   _____

5. Mason said he wanted just one bite, but only a **fraction** of it was left.

   _____

6. The smell coming from the garbage bag was so **horrid** that I held my nose as I carried it to the dumpster.

   _____

7. Because Madeline worked the math problems with such **haste**, she made several careless mistakes.

   _____

8. The new governor's speech had few new ideas. It merely **echoed** the ideas of the previous governor.

   _____

9. The room was not **vacant**, so there was no place to hold the meeting.

   _____

10. Peter is known to **exaggerate** about the size of the fish he catches.

   _____

WORD MEANINGS

Word Learning—Group A

Study the spelling, part(s) of speech, and meaning(s) of each word from Group A. Complete each sentence by writing the word on the line. Then read the sentence.

1. **accuse** *(v.)* to charge someone with doing something wrong

   Amy pointed to the man to _____ him of stealing her sister's purse.

2. **compass** *(n.)* an instrument used to determine direction, having a needle that points north

   Use a map and _____ to guide you northward.

3. **complain** *(v.)* 1. to say that something is wrong or troublesome; 2. to find fault

   It does no good to _____ about bad weather.

4. **disappoint** *(v.)* to fail to satisfy one's hope or wish

   If the band fails to show up, they will _____ their fans.

5. **exaggerate** *(v.)* to say that something is more than it is

   That reporter tends to _____ what he reports.

6. **independence** *(n.)* freedom from the control or help of others

   The rebels struggled for their _____ from the dictator.

7. **masquerade** *(v.)* 1. to wear a mask or disguise; 2. to go about as if in disguise; *(n.)* a costume party at which masks are worn

   The thieves plan to _____ as police officers.

   No one will guess who you are at the _____ party.

8. **melody** *(n.)* a sequence of single tones in a piece of music

   Adriana keeps humming that well-known _____ she heard on the radio.

9. sanitary *(adj.)* free from germs, dirt, and filth

The cleaning staff was praised for the _____ condition of the hospital rooms.

10. vacant *(adj.)* containing nothing; empty

The neighbors plan to build a park in the _____ lot.

Use Your Vocabulary—Group A

Choose the word from Group A that best completes each sentence. Write the word on the line. You may use the plural form of nouns and the past tense of verbs if necessary.

My buddy Liam and I __1__ all the time about being the youngest in our families. So we decided to show our __2__ from our older brothers and sisters. We don't need them! Mom said we could camp out alone in the __3__ lot behind my house. "Camping is not __4__!" sniffed my big sister, "There's no shower out there." Liam's big brother jeered, "You'd better take my __5__ so you can find your way home from the backyard."

That night I heard an odd noise. I __6__ Liam of snoring like a bear. "You always __7__," Liam grumbled. He peeked outside. There was his big brother, trying to __8__ as a bear. We laughed and came out of the tent, whistling a happy __9__. "Aw, gee," Liam's brother mumbled. "You weren't even a little scared." He tried to look __10__, but I think he really was proud of us.

1. _____

2. _____

3. _____

4. _____

5. _____

6. _____

7. _____

8. _____

9. _____

10. _____

Vocabulary in Action

The first four letters in **masquerade** are pronounced just like *mask*, which one might wear as a disguise. This may help you recall that *masquerade*, when used as a verb, means "to wear a mask or disguise."

Word Learning—Group B

Study the spelling, part(s) of speech, and meaning(s) of each word from Group B. Complete each sentence by writing the word on the line. Then read the sentence.

1. **campaign** *(v.)* to seek election votes; *(n.)* a plan or series of connected activities done to get something

   "I will _____ for the current mayor," said the volunteer.

   The mayor headed the clean-up _____ and improved our community.

2. **disarrange** *(v.)* to put out of order

   A two-car accident is likely to _____ the headlights on both cars.

3. **echo** *(n.)* a repeated sound; *(v.)* to repeat or imitate

   Give a yell and listen to the _____ in these granite hills.

   Squawker, my parrot, will _____ any word you say.

4. **fault** *(n.)* 1. a mistake or an error; 2. responsibility for failure

   Who is at _____ for this broken window?

5. **fraction** *(n.)* 1. a part of a whole; 2. not all of a thing

   The sports store discounted the hockey sticks to a _____ of the original price.

6. **haste** *(n.)* a quick or hurried action

   In their _____, they forgot their airplane tickets.

7. **horrid** *(adj.)* very unpleasant

   Is that _____ smell coming from the chemistry lab?

8. **justice** *(n.)* fairness; rightness

   The judge's sense of _____ ensures the man will get a fair trial.

9. latitude *(n.)* 1. distance from equator; 2. freedom of choice or action

The _____ of the island of Trinidad is on line with Caracas, Venezuela.

Alexis gave her employees great _____ in making decisions for themselves.

10. magnetize *(v.)* 1. to make magnetic; 2. to attract or influence a person

Our science teacher showed us how to _____ a piece of iron so that it will attract metal filings.

Use Your Vocabulary—Group B

Choose the word from Group B that best completes each sentence. Write the word on the line. You may use the plural form of nouns and the past tense of verbs if necessary.

Drew Devlin's **1** to become the next president of the United States was in trouble. Although popular in the Southern states, only a small **2** of the voters in the North supported him. With only two weeks before the election, Devlin traveled in **3** to the North to make speeches. He gave his speechwriters great **4** in their choice of campaign issues. "Just get me the votes," he said. The main points the writers always covered were

- the **5** , troubling crime problem
- **6** and fairness for all people
- correcting **7** in the legal system.

Devlin **8** the voters with his clear message of reform, attracting more and more of their support. Many of his statements **9** the voters' feelings. Then just before the election, the polls showed that the order of candidate standings was **10** . Devlin had taken the lead.

1. _____

2. _____

3. _____

4. _____

5. _____

6. _____

7. _____

8. _____

9. _____

10. _____

SYNONYMS

Synonyms are words that have the same or nearly the same meanings.

Part 1 Choose the word from the box that is the best synonym for each group of words. Write the word on the line.

sanitary	fault	justice	complain	magnetize
melody	horrid	accuse	disarrange	exaggerate

1. goodness, honesty, fair play _____

2. sterile, clean, spotless _____

3. guilt, blame, flaw _____

4. magnify, boast, overdo _____

5. express displeasure, criticize, gripe _____

6. persuade, fascinate, charm _____

7. scramble, mix up, upset, jumble _____

8. sickening, awful, gruesome, horrible _____

9. lodge a complaint against, blame, indict _____

10. song, ballad, tune _____

Vocabulary in Action

An **echo** is usually caused when the waves made by a sound bounce off a flat surface. It is similar to the way light bounces off a mirror. Our word *echo* comes from Greek mythology. The nymph Echo was cursed by a goddess so that she could only repeat what other people said. She fell in love with a young man named Narcissus. Because of her curse, she could not explain herself. When Narcissus left, she hid herself and faded away until only her voice was left.

Part 2 Replace the underlined word(s) with a word from the box that means the same or almost the same. Write your answer on the line.

vacant	independence	campaign	haste	masquerade
latitude	disappoint	echo	compass	fraction

11. The candidate will <u>dishearten</u> his supporters if he withdraws from the race. _____

12. Paul Revere rode with <u>swiftness</u> to warn of the approaching British. _____

13. The Sonoran Desert may look <u>uninhabited</u>, but many creatures live there.

_____

14. The money I earned shoveling snow is just a <u>portion</u> of what I expected to earn. _____

15. The language teacher instructed the class to <u>repeat back</u> each Spanish word. _____

16. The tiny island government's <u>liberty</u> was assured by its strong army.

_____

17. In a <u>huge effort</u> to make the city beautiful, volunteers planted 12,000 flowers. _____

18. Whom did you dress as for the <u>costume party</u>? _____

19. North, south, east, and west are marked on this <u>device to indicate directions</u>. _____

20. Ahoy, ships at sea, please radio in your <u>position</u>. _____

 **ANTONYMS**

Antonyms are words that have opposite or nearly opposite meanings.

Part 1 Choose the word from the box that is the best antonym for each group of words. Write the word on the line.

echo	masquerade	magnetize	accuse
fraction	haste	independence	complain

1. whole amount, complete object _____

2. said only once; differ from _____

3. show oneself, reveal _____

4. defend, pardon, stick up for _____

5. slowness, delay _____

6. compliment, praise, approve _____

7. slavery, lack of liberty _____

8. repel, push away, repulse _____

Part 2 Replace the underlined word with a word from the box that means the opposite or almost the opposite. Write your answer on the line.

fault	horrid	justice	sanitary
disappoint	exaggerates	vacant	disarrange

9. The water in this bottle looks <u>dirty</u>. Do you think it's OK to drink?

_____

10. Whenever Grandfather tells a war story, he always <u>understates</u> his role

in the victory. _____

11. When you serve lima beans, you <u>please</u> everyone in the family.

_____

12. There's nothing like the <u>pleasant</u> odor of an opossum living under your porch. _____

13. After the movie premier, the star was surprised to see a <u>crowded</u> theater lobby. _____

14. Take a moment to <u>organize</u> your drawer. _____

15. Would you expect <u>dishonesty</u> to play a role in this crime?

_____

16. The <u>credit</u> for the look of our bedroom is my brother's, not mine.

_____

WORD STUDY

Prefixes Complete each sentence with a word from the box that means the opposite or nearly the opposite of the underlined word(s).

react	replace	recall	reuse	rebuild

1. Don't <u>throw out</u> that paper. I was going to _____ it.

2. After the tornado, the homeowners decided to <u>tear down</u> the damaged house and _____ it.

3. I wish I could <u>forget</u> the worst game of my life, but actually I _____ the game perfectly.

4. Should we buy more cereal to _____ what we used or leave the pantry shelf <u>empty</u>?

5. <u>Ignore</u> the jeers of the other team's fans because if you _____, they will yell louder.

CHALLENGE WORDS

Word Learning—Challenge!

Study the spelling, part(s) of speech, and meaning(s) of each word.
Complete each sentence by writing the word on the line. Then read the
sentence.

1. compose *(v.)* 1. to make up; 2. to form by putting together; 3. to make calm

Didn't Beethoven _____ nine symphonies?

2. inaugurate *(v.)* 1. to install in office with a ceremony; 2. to bring about the beginning of with a ceremony

I believe that we _____ the president in January.

3. pallor *(n.)* 1. lack of color from fear, illness, or death; 2. paleness

From the _____ on your face, I can tell you don't feel well.

4. periodical *(n.)* 1. a magazine that is published at regular times; 2. not daily

National Geographic is a _____ that comes out every month.

5. relent *(v.)* 1. to become less harsh; 2. to let up; 3. to soften

I'll _____ this time and let you stay out later.

Use Your Vocabulary—Challenge!

My Magazine You are the editor of a new political magazine. The first
issue is coming out in two weeks. On a separate sheet of paper, write
a radio ad for your magazine using the Challenge Words above. Be
sure to tell what your magazine is about, the election stories you are
covering, and how much it costs. Try to make it sound so fascinating that
anyone hearing your ad will want to buy your magazine.

Donovan discovers that a fierce storm has smashed his box of words. Help him put his words back together. Combine the broken groups of letters to form words and match each word with its definition. Each piece may be used only once.

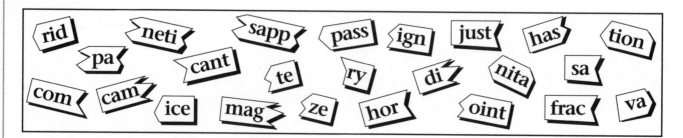

1. A place that is empty is _____.

2. This word stands for fairness: _____.

3. If you let someone down, you _____ that person.

4. People who rush are in _____.

5. If you can attract others, you can _____ people.

6. An area that is free of germs is _____.

7. This device points north: _____.

8. If you don't have the whole amount of something, then you have a

   _____ of it.

9. Places that are very unpleasant are _____.

10. A candidate seeking to get elected is sure to run a large

    _____.

Review 5-6

WORD MEANINGS

Fill in the bubble of the word that is best defined by each phrase.

1. a sound that is heard again
   (a.) echo   (b.) foundation   (c.) vapor   (d.) whine

2. to not satisfy a dream or wish
   (a.) defrost   (b.) campaign   (c.) complain   (d.) disappoint

3. what you might need on a journey
   (a.) latitude   (b.) compass   (c.) masquerade   (d.) easel

4. to warm up
   (a.) defrost   (b.) exaggerate   (c.) disarrange   (d.) dispute

5. where objects are collected and displayed
   (a.) masquerade   (b.) gland   (c.) museum   (d.) compass

6. spotlessly clean
   (a.) horrid   (b.) vacant   (c.) foreign   (d.) sanitary

7. an angry argument
   (a.) fraction   (b.) independence   (c.) dispute   (d.) melody

8. to tell what's going to happen
   (a.) magnetize   (b.) disarrange   (c.) forecast   (d.) complain

9. can be seen only with a microscope
   (a.) bacteria   (b.) banquet   (c.) justice   (d.) dungeon

10. used to measure
    (a.) echo   (b.) gauge   (c.) compass   (d.) easel

11. having space available
    (a.) sanitary   (b.) horrid   (c.) vacant   (d.) flexible

12. an underground prison
    (a.) museum   (b.) dungeon   (c.) plateau   (d.) masquerade

13. a bunch of something
    (a.) echo   (b.) batch   (c.) melody   (d.) latitude

14. to cry in a childish way
    (a.) whine   (b.) disappoint   (c.) accuse   (d.) dispute

15. very bad
    (a.) vacant   (b.) desirable   (c.) horrid   (d.) sanitary

SENTENCE COMPLETION

Choose the word from Part 1 that best completes each of the following sentences. Write the word in the blank. Then do the same for Part 2. You will not use all the words.

Part 1

paralyzed	masquerade	flexible	melody
desirable	complained	exaggerated	plateau

1. Certain types of cacti cannot survive on a valley floor and can only grow high on a(n) _____.

2. After ten years of gymnastics lessons, Ryan was so _____ that he could touch the back of his head with his toes.

3. I found the _____ catchy, but the song's lyrics bored me.

4. When I honked the horn, the dog became _____ with fear, and his owner had to carry him away.

5. I _____ when I saw that my sister got more cake than I did.

Part 2

foreign	horrid	fault	campaign
magnetize	operation	justice	haste

6. The Spartans' military _____ was so well planned that they won the war within weeks.

7. Austin was supposed to bring the grill, so it is his _____ nobody is eating hot dogs for dinner.

8. The visiting student's sense of humor was so _____ to me that I could not understand her jokes at all.

9. In their _____ to reach the football game before kickoff, the Andersons accidentally left the car lights on.

10. Once I figured out that a battery controlled the _____ of the clock, I easily fixed it.

Posttest

CHOOSING THE DEFINITIONS

Fill in the bubble of the item that best defines the word in bold.

1. My best friend is the most **dependable** person I know.
   (a.) messy   (b.) trustworthy   (c.) kind   (d.) faraway

2. The watch Grandpa gave me is very **precious** to me.
   (a.) old   (b.) cheap   (c.) pretty   (d.) special

3. Garbage in a compost pile will **decay** over time.
   (a.) ripen   (b.) grow   (c.) rot   (d.) shrink

4. Losing the camera was not Brianna's **fault.**
   (a.) error   (b.) accomplishment   (c.) idea   (d.) excuse

5. Resources such as oil are becoming more **scarce.**
   (a.) plentiful   (b.) extinct   (c.) rare   (d.) common

6. Pulling weeds can form a **callus** on your hand.
   (a.) cut   (b.) hard skin   (c.) rash   (d.) bruise

7. The fierce pirate sent the prisoner to the **dungeon.**
   (a.) prison   (b.) auditorium   (c.) ocean   (d.) attic

8. Dad hired a truck to **transport** our furniture to the new house.
   (a.) leave   (b.) lift   (c.) report   (d.) carry

9. Being in an accident is a **horrid** experience.
   (a.) pleasant   (b.) dramatic   (c.) unpleasant   (d.) exciting

10. I get an allowance so I can learn about **financial** matters.
    (a.) about work   (b.) about money   (c.) about wisdom   (d.) about art

11. The new baby's room looked bright, cheerful, and **sanitary.**
    (a.) pretty   (b.) clean   (c.) dirty   (d.) colorful

12. The mayor made an **objection** to the new law.
    (a.) argument   (b.) agreement   (c.) addition   (d.) promise

13. The little fawn stood very still, **paralyzed** by our bright flashlight.
    (a.) stunned   (b.) frightened   (c.) angered   (d.) excited

14. It was hard to **gauge** how much food to make.
    (a.) prepare   (b.) poke   (c.) estimate   (d.) feel

15. When the hot sun came out, the water in the puddle **evaporated.**
 (a.) darkened (b.) dried up (c.) froze (d.) spilled

16. It does no good to **complain** about the weather.
 (a.) criticize (b.) praise (c.) dislike (d.) enjoy

17. Megan made a **pledge** to walk the new puppy every day.
 (a.) habit (b.) story (c.) promise (d.) speech

18. Everyone wants to be treated with **respect.**
 (a.) consideration (b.) dishonor (c.) glory (d.) caution

19. Victoria wants to learn to be a **surgeon** just like her mother.
 (a.) plumber (b.) doctor (c.) teacher (d.) lawyer

20. Until we got to know him, the new student seemed **bashful.**
 (a.) handsome (b.) loud (c.) smart (d.) shy

21. The strong wind made the fallen leaves **whirl** around.
 (a.) spin (b.) drop (c.) run (d.) bounce

22. I may have **exaggerated** the story of my touchdown a little.
 (a.) told (b.) written (c.) made larger (d.) narrowed

23. The American patriots fought for independence and **liberty.**
 (a.) honor (b.) freedom (c.) money (d.) pride

24. It took time for the ice on the car window to **defrost.**
 (a.) freeze (b.) melt (c.) harden (d.) leave

25. The two girls found a **satisfactory** solution to their problem.
 (a.) quick (b.) useless (c.) good enough (d.) very bad

26. Our team should not have **accused** the other team of cheating.
 (a.) blamed (b.) arrested (c.) avoided (d.) fought

27. Everyone liked the president's **sensible** plan.
 (a.) silly (b.) boring (c.) financial (d.) reasonable

28. William said I tripped him, but I was **innocent.**
 (a.) sleeping (b.) not guilty (c.) unhappy (d.) quiet

29. The boss praised Emma for being a **capable** worker.
 (a.) lazy (b.) fit (c.) pleasant (d.) well-paid

30. The workers built a **canal** to connect the two lakes.
 (a.) waterway (b.) highway (c.) railway (d.) airline

USING CONTEXT CLUES

Use the word in bold and the sentence context to figure out the phrase that best completes each sentence. Fill in the bubble for your answer.

31. You may hear an **echo** when you

    (a.) sing in a field.

    (b.) talk to another person.

    (c.) shout in a cave.

    (d.) dance in the wind.

32. If you think something is **desirable**, you

    (a.) do not like its taste.

    (b.) wish you could have it.

    (c.) give it away.

    (d.) think it is ugly.

33. When you look at the **galaxy**, you are

    (a.) looking down.

    (b.) looking into a river.

    (c.) always wearing dark glasses.

    (d.) usually looking at the night sky.

34. If you visit a **foreign** country, you

    (a.) are probably far from home.

    (b.) are in your own neighborhood.

    (c.) are visiting your state capital.

    (d.) will see familiar things.

35. A **compass** can help you

    (a.) tell the correct time.

    (b.) measure a long distance.

    (c.) find your way home.

    (d.) forecast the weather.

36. When you pledge **allegiance**, you

    (a.) tell a lie.

    (b.) promise to be loyal.

    (c.) sing about your country.

    (d.) promise to pay back what you owe.

37. A person who works as an **usher**

    (a.) shows people where to sit.

    (b.) buys and sells goods for a living.

    (c.) performs an operation.

    (d.) repairs cars.

38. A person offers **hospitality** by

    (a.) curing a serious illness.

    (b.) not answering the door.

    (c.) refusing to share.

    (d.) inviting you to come in.

39. If you lose a **molar**, you should visit

a. a teacher.

b. the police.

c. a dentist.

d. the dog pound.

40. If you travel across the **equator**, you may be traveling between

a. New York and Los Angeles.

b. North and South America.

c. the United States and Canada.

d. California and Florida.

41. An **obedient** pet

a. follows your directions.

b. chews up your shoes.

c. sleeps most of the day.

d. lives in a cage.

42. An **industrious** person

a. is always nervous.

b. is usually lazy.

c. talks too loudly.

d. works very hard.

43. A place with a good **climate** has

a. a good police department.

b. many landmarks.

c. nice weather.

d. independence.

44. A person who ate a **batch** of cookies would probably

a. still be hungry.

b. feel sick.

c. be very healthy.

d. be very thin.

45. When you **compare** two things, you

a. measure and weigh both things.

b. choose one thing or the other.

c. spend time with both things.

d. tell how they are alike and different.

46. **Justice** has been done when

a. a problem is settled fairly.

b. someone is punished.

c. someone is arrested.

d. your team is the winner.

47. Wild animals chase their **prey** because they

a. need to have fun.

b. want to have company.

c. need to have food.

d. want to get exercise.

48. An **impatient** person would be unhappy if

    a. the music was too loud.   **c.** the room was dirty

    b. the food was burned.   **d.** the train was late.

49. You could find a **gland**

    a. at an antique show.   **c.** in a computer store.

    b. in your own body.   **d.** in an office.

50. The main job of a shoe **manufacturer** is to

    a. wear shoes.   **c.** destroy shoes.

    b. buy shoes.   **d.** make shoes.

51. An award for **conduct** is given for

    a. artistic talent.   **c.** good handwriting.

    b. good behavior.   **d.** athletic ability.

52. **Bacteria** are closest in size to

    a. grains of rice.   **c.** specks of dust.

    b. goldfish.   **d.** seeds.

53. To see your **reflection**, you would look at a

    a. mirror.   **c.** chalkboard.

    b. scale.   **d.** watch.

54. You would learn about **latitude** in

    a. music class.   **c.** gym class.

    b. English class.   **d.** geography class.

55. You can see the **horizon** if there are

    a. fluffy clouds in the sky.   **c.** very tall trees around you.

    b. no buildings in your way.   **d.** many people with you.

56. If someone **escorts** you, that person

    a. hits you.   **c.** asks you a question.

    b. sings to you.   **d.** goes with you.

57. The state **capital** is

    a. a bird.   **c.** a flower.

    b. a letter in the state's name.   **d.** a city.

58. One example of **vapor** is

    a. fog in the air.   **c.** ice on a pond.

    b. water in a river.   **d.** milk in a glass.

59. A bathtub that is filled to **capacity** is

    a. overflowing.   **c.** half full.

    b. filled to the very top.   **d.** empty.

60. If an object has been **magnetized**, it will pick up

    a. plastic toys.   **c.** iron nails.

    b. spilled water.   **d.** fallen leaves.

61. If you feel a **draft**, you will be

    a. hungry.   **c.** scared.

    b. happier.   **d.** cooler.

62. You perform an act of **charity** when you

    a. collect food for others.   **c.** buy new clothes for yourself.

    b. play in the school band.   **d.** do your homework.

63. **Insulation** in your home keeps you

    a. dry during a rainstorm.   **c.** from running out of food.

    b. warm in the winter.   **d.** from going outdoors.

64. An **easel** is often used by

    a. a doctor.   **c.** an artist.

    b. a mechanic.   **d.** a chef.

65. An **eternal** flame will

    a. never go out.   **c.** be very hot.

    b. burn out quickly.   **d.** start a forest fire.

Test-Taking Tips

Taking a standardized test can be difficult. Here are a few things you can do to make the experience easier.

Get a good night's sleep the night before the test. You want to be alert and rested in the morning.

Eat a healthful breakfast. Your brain needs good food to work properly.

Wear layers of clothing. You can take off or put on a layer if you get too warm or too cold.

Bring two sharp number 2 pencils with erasers.

When you get the test, read the directions carefully. Be sure you understand what you are supposed to do. If you have any questions, ask your teacher before you start marking your answers.

If you feel nervous, close your eyes and take a deep breath as you silently count to three. Then slowly breathe out. Do this several times until your mind is calm.

Manage your time. Check to see how many questions there are. Try to answer half the questions before half the time is up.

Answer the easy questions first. If you don't know the answer to a question, skip it and come back to it later if you have time.

Try to answer all the questions. Some will seem very hard, but don't worry about it. Nobody is expected to get every answer right. Make the best guess you can.

If you make a mistake, erase it completely. Then write the correct answer or fill in the correct circle.

When you have finished, go back over the test. Work on any questions you skipped. Check your answers.

Question Types

Many tests contain the same kinds of questions. Here are a few of the question types that you may encounter.

Meaning from Context

This kind of question asks you to figure out the meaning of a word from the words or sentences around it.

> The smoke from the smoldering garbage made her eyes water.

Which word in the sentence helps you understand the meaning of *smoldering*?

smoke	garbage
eyes	water

Read the sentence carefully. You know that smoke comes from something that is burning. *Smoldering* must mean "burning." *Smoke* is the correct answer.

Synonyms and Antonyms

Some questions ask you to identify the synonym of a word. Synonyms are words that have the same or nearly the same meaning. Some questions ask you to identify the antonym of a word. Antonyms are words that have the opposite or nearly the opposite meaning.

> The workers buffed the statue until it shone like a mirror.

Which word is a synonym for *buffed*?

polished   covered

tarnished   dismantled

Read the answers carefully. Which word means "to make something shine"? The answer is *polish*.

> When she feels morose, she watches funny cartoons to change her mood.

Which word is an antonym of *morose*?

dismal   agreeable

happy   confident

Think about the sentence. If something funny will change her mood, she must be sad. The answer is *happy*, the antonym of *sad*.

Analogies

This kind of question asks you to find relationships between pairs of words. Analogies usually use *is to* and *as*.

> **green** is to **grass** as _____ is to **sky**

Green is the color of grass. So the answer must be **blue**, the color of the sky.

Roots

A root is a building block for words. Many roots come from ancient languages such as Greek or Latin. Knowing the meaning of a root can often help you figure out the meaning of a word. Note that sometimes the spelling of the root changes.

Root	Language	Meaning	Example
audi	Latin	to hear	audience audible auditorium
bibl	Greek	book	bibliography Bible bibliophile
cred	Latin	to believe	credence creed incredible
dict	Greek	to speak	predict dictionary dictation
finis	Latin	end, limit	finish finally infinite
graph	Greek	to write or draw	autograph biography paragraph
scribe	Latin	to write	describe subscribe prescribe

Prefixes

A prefix is a word part added to the beginning of a base word. A prefix changes the meaning of the base word.

Prefix	Meaning	Base Word	Example
dis-	not, opposite of	like	dislike
mid-	in the middle of	air	midair
mis-	badly, wrongly	behave	misbehave
pre-	before, earlier	cook	precook
re-	again	paint	repaint
sub-	under	freezing	subfreezing
tele-	far away	photo	telephoto
un-	not	happy	unhappy
under-	below, less than	foot	underfoot

Suffixes

Suffixes

A suffix is a word part added to the end of a base word. A suffix changes the meaning of the base word. Sometimes the base word changes spelling when a suffix is added.

Suffix	Meaning	Base Word	Example
-able	able to be, full of	agree	agreeable
-al	relating to	music	musical
-ate	to make	active	activate
-en	to become, to make	light	lighten
-er	person who	teach	teacher
		run	runner
-ful	full of	cheer	cheerful
		beauty	beautiful
-fy	to make	simple	simplify
-ic	like a, relating to	artist	artistic
		athlete	athletic
-ish	like a, resembling	child	childish
-ize	to cause to be	legal	legalize
		apology	apologize
-less	without	hope	hopeless
		penny	penniless
-ly, -ally	in a (certain) way	sad	sadly
		magic	magically
-ship	a state of being	friend	friendship
-ward	in the direction of	east	eastward
-y	like, full of	thirst	thirsty
		fog	foggy

My Vocabulary in Action Dictionary

Categories: *Individual, Visual Learners*

Create your own dictionary of vocabulary words. Take 14 sheets of white paper and one sheet of construction paper and fold them in half. Place the white paper inside the folded construction paper to create a book. Staple the book together on the fold. Label each page of your book with one letter of the alphabet.

At the end of each vocabulary chapter, enter the new words into your dictionary. Include the word, the definition, the part of speech, and a sentence. Each definition should be written in your own words. This will be a good tool to use throughout the year.

Vocabulary Challenge

Category: *Small Group*

Prepare for the game by choosing 15 vocabulary words from the current chapter. Write each word on a separate index card. On the back of the card, write the definition of the word. Place the cards on the floor, with the definition-side down, in three rows of five cards.

Three or four players sit facing the cards. The first player points to a word and gives its definition. If the player gives the correct definition, he or she gets to keep the card. If the player gives the wrong definition, he or she returns the card to the floor.

Players take turns until all the cards are gone. The player with the most cards wins the game.

Vocabulary Quilt

Categories: *Individual or Small Group, Visual Learners*

Find one or two friends to help create a "vocabulary quilt," or create a quilt of your own. Write each vocabulary word from the current chapter in big letters across the top of a separate sheet of construction paper. Illustrate each word, using markers or colored pencils. As you finish, place the pictures in a quilt-like arrangement on a bulletin board. Leave the pictures posted in the room and allow the other students to "visually" learn their vocabulary words.

Toss the Ball

Categories: *Small Group, Kinesthetic Learners*

Find four friends and sit in a circle on the floor. Your group will need a ball and a list of the current chapter's vocabulary words. The first person with the ball says a vocabulary word aloud, then quickly tosses the ball to another person in the group. That person must correctly define the word. If successful, that person says another vocabulary word and tosses the ball to another player. If the word is not defined correctly, the player must leave the circle. The game continues until there is only one player remaining.

For an additional challenge, say a synonym or an antonym for the word instead of a definition.

Synonym Partners

Category: *Large Group*

Write the current chapter's vocabulary words on index cards. Then write a synonym for each word on additional cards. Divide the class into two groups and give the words to one group and the synonyms to the other group.

The object of the game is for each student to find the appropriate synonym partner without speaking or using body language. The partners sit on the floor once they find each other. After all partners are found, each pair tells the class the vocabulary word, its synonym, and the definition.

This game may also be played using an antonym of the vocabulary word instead of a synonym. For a greater challenge, play the game using both a synonym and an antonym without using the vocabulary word.

Catch That Plate

Categories: *Small Group, Kinesthetic Learners*

Write the vocabulary words from the current chapter on slips of paper and place them in a hat. Ask the players to sit in a circle on the floor. Place the hat and a plastic plate in the center. The first player goes to the center of the circle, takes a slip of paper, reads the word, names another player, and spins the plate. The player whose name was called must quickly give a definition for the vocabulary word and then "catch the plate" before it comes to a stop. If successful, that player becomes the new plate spinner. If that player fails to catch the plate in time, the same plate spinner remains.

Vocabulary Egg Shake

Category: *Partners, Kinesthetic Learners*

Find a partner and write the current chapter's vocabulary words on slips of paper. Glue these slips to the inside of each cup section of an egg carton. Place a penny in the egg carton and close the carton. The first partner shakes the carton and then lifts the lid. The second partner must state the correct definition of the vocabulary word on which the penny landed. If successful, he or she must shake the carton. For a variation to this game, state the synonym or antonym for the vocabulary word instead of the definition.

This activity can be used for each new vocabulary chapter by replacing the vocabulary words with new words.

Vocabulary Search

Categories: *Small Group,*
Kinesthetic Learners,
ELL

Form a group of five students. Create alphabet cards from cardboard. Cut out 75 small squares and write one letter of the alphabet on each square. Make two alphabets plus several additional squares for each vowel.

Place the alphabet squares in two piles —with the same letters in each pile—in the middle of the playing area. Designate one person to be the announcer. The remaining four players break into teams of two. The game begins when the announcer says a definition, a synonym, or an antonym of one of the current chapter's vocabulary words. Then each team uses the alphabet cards to try to spell the word to which the announcer is referring. The first team to correctly spell the word receives one point. The team with the most points at the end of the game wins.

Vocabulary Baseball

Category: *Small Group*

Prepare for the game by drawing a baseball diamond on a sheet of paper. Be sure to include three bases and home plate. Write on index cards all of the current chapter's vocabulary words, along with their definitions. Find three friends and divide into two teams. Determine how many innings there will be in the game.

The first team at bat sends its player to home plate. The first player on the other team "pitches" a word to the batter by reading a word. If the batter correctly states the definition, he or she moves to first base. The player continues to move from base to base until he or she crosses home plate or misses the definition. When a player misses, the team gets an out. After three outs, the other team is at bat.

When a player crosses home plate, the team gets one point and the next player bats. The team with the most points at the end of the last inning wins the game.

Vocabulary Fables

Categories: *Individual,*
**   Visual Learners*

Reread a popular fairy tale, such as "Cinderella" or "The Three Little Pigs." After you have finished reading the story, write your own version, using at least 10 vocabulary words from the current chapter. Make your new story into a book with illustrated pages and a construction-paper cover. Share your story with your classmates or with another class.

Comic-Strip Vocabulary

Categories: *Individual,*
**   Visual Learners*

Prepare for the game by bringing to class some examples of comic strips from newspapers or magazines. Look over the examples for ideas to create your own comic strip. You can either make up new comic-strip characters or use existing characters. Fold a sheet of paper into six equal parts to create six frames. Use at least four of the current chapter's vocabulary words in your story. You should fill each frame with words and pictures. You might display your comic strip or share it with classmates.

Vocabulary Tic-Tac-Toe

Category: *Partners*

Prepare for the game by writing the current chapter's vocabulary words on index cards. Write the definition of the word on the back of the card. You will also need to create five *X* and five *O* cards. Place the vocabulary cards, definition-side down, in a stack. Draw a large tic-tac-toe board on a sheet of paper. Cover each square with a vocabulary card, definition-side down.

Work with a partner. The first player chooses a word and says the definition. If the player is correct, he or she removes the card and replaces it with an *X*. If the player is incorrect, the card goes to the bottom of the vocabulary stack and is replaced with a new card. Then the second player chooses a word and tries to define it. The game continues until a player has successfully made a "tic-tac-toe." This game can be played many times by shuffling the vocabulary cards between rounds.

Word Search Puzzles

Categories: *Partners, Auditory Learners*

Prepare for the game by bringing to class examples of word search puzzles from newspapers, magazines, or books. You will need one sheet of graph paper and a pencil. Use the examples to guide you in creating a word search puzzle that includes some of the vocabulary words from the current chapter. On another sheet of paper, write the definitions of the words you included.

When you have finished your word search puzzle, exchange it with a friend. Take turns reading aloud your definition clues. Your partner must guess the correct vocabulary word and find it in your word search puzzle. Return the word search puzzle to the appropriate owner to check for accuracy.

Tell Me a Story

Category: *Small Group*

Find three partners. You will need two sheets of paper and a pen or pencil. Write all the vocabulary words from the current chapter on one sheet of notebook paper.

One person in the group begins creating a story by writing a sentence or two, using one of the vocabulary words. That person then passes the paper to the next group member. Each player is allowed to use only one vocabulary word each turn. The object of the game is to use all the vocabulary words correctly to form a complete story. The story must make sense, and it must have a beginning, a middle, and an end. Ask someone to check your story for accuracy.

Vocabulary Role-Play

Categories: *Small Group, Kinesthetic Learners, ELL*

Find two partners. Pick 15 vocabulary words from the current chapter. Write each word on a separate small slip of paper. Fold the slips of paper in half and place them in a hat.

Each person selects a word from the hat. When it's your turn, take two minutes to develop a short skit about your word to perform for your partners. In the skit, you must act out your vocabulary word without saying the word. The first person to guess the word correctly draws the next word.

Jeopardy

Categories: *Small Group, Auditory Learners*

Work with three partners. One player starts by giving the definition of a current chapter's vocabulary word. The other three players try to guess the word as quickly as possible. (They do not have to wait for the entire definition.) The first one to guess the word correctly gets to give the next definition. Keep track of who correctly guesses the most words.

Words in Context

Categories: *Partners,*
Technology,
ELL

Work with a partner at a computer. One person enters a vocabulary word from the current chapter. Then the second person enters a sentence using that word correctly. Take turns entering words and sentences. See how many you can complete in 10 minutes. (If you do not have access to a computer, you can write the words and sentences on a sheet of paper.)

Concentration

Categories: *Partners,*
Visual Learners,
ELL

Write eight of the current chapter's vocabulary words on separate index cards. Write the definitions of the words on eight more index cards. Shuffle the cards and place them facedown in a square with four rows of four cards.

Work with a partner. One person turns over two cards. If the definition matches the word, that player keeps the cards. If the definition does not match the word, the player puts the cards facedown in the same places they were before. The other player then turns over two cards. Continue until all the cards have been taken. The partner with the most pairs of cards wins the game.